Wax in the D

An Exhibition of Encaustic Art

Curated by Candace Law

The artwork in this catalog was created by Detroit-area artists and shown in an exhibition of encaustic art curated by visual artist Candace Law at the Village Theater in Canton, Michigan, during February 2017.

———

Published by folioDetroit™. Visit folioDetroit.com for more information about our services or to purchase copies of this and other publications.

Cover photograph by Melissa Rian
Artwork photographs by the artist (Christina Czaja and Kate Paul) or Eric Law / ShootMyArt.com

ISBN-13: 978-1542355513
ISBN-10: 1542355516

"The job of the artist is always
to deepen the mystery."
—Francis Bacon

"Creativity is inventing, experimenting, growing, taking risks, breaking rules, making mistakes, and having fun."
—Mary Lou Cook

Curator's Statement

Encaustic is a wonderful medium that is being discovered by artists in increasing numbers. Or, rather, re-discovered, because it actually dates back to ancient Greece. Wax was used to waterproof their ships, as well as by artisans, and it has been in and out of favor in fine art through the centuries since. More recently, it was artist Jasper Johns who helped bring encaustic onto the contemporary art scene in the heyday of the Abstract Expressionists. He came across this little-known medium and was taken with its possibilities. As he worked out his own mixtures and processes, Johns created stunning bodies of work that are in major collections and still on display today.

In its simplest form, encaustic is a combination of beeswax, a little damar resin, and pigment. The mixture is brought to a molten state and applied with a brush to a rigid surface while still liquid. Once it has cooled, this top surface is reheated so the wax melts into the layers beneath. It is this layering that gives an encaustic piece its unique depth and luminosity, as well as allowing for interleaving other materials that make it so versatile. As I came to this exquisite medium, I was taken with both the visual beauty it produces and the very tactile feel of the surface.

In an era of rapidly changing technology—where so many things are not permanent—working with a process that connects me to artists from millennia past grounds me as an artist and has made me a champion for the medium. I started to offer workshops to encourage experimenting with this beguiling art form. In the process of working with other artists, our time together has become as much about sharing our creative talent and energy with each other as learning new techniques. It is a natural next step, then, to show this medium and what it can be within the larger art community.

My goal in curating this exhibition is to promote a growing awareness of encaustic and to showcase artists who are successfully expanding their vision and their craft by pursuing this challenging art form. It has been an honor and a pleasure to bring this group together and show my work alongside theirs.

Candace Law
January 2017

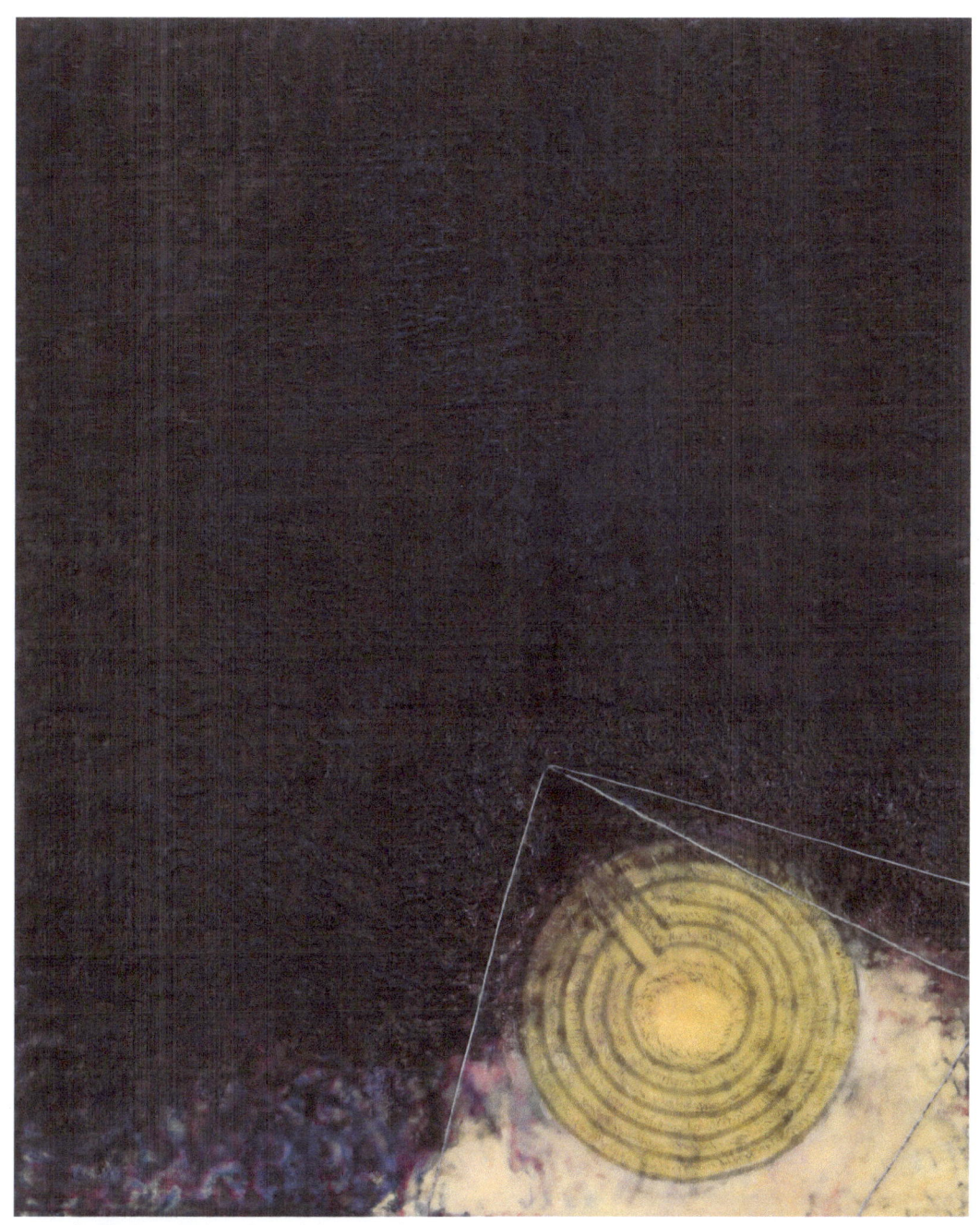

Candace Law | Night of the Soul

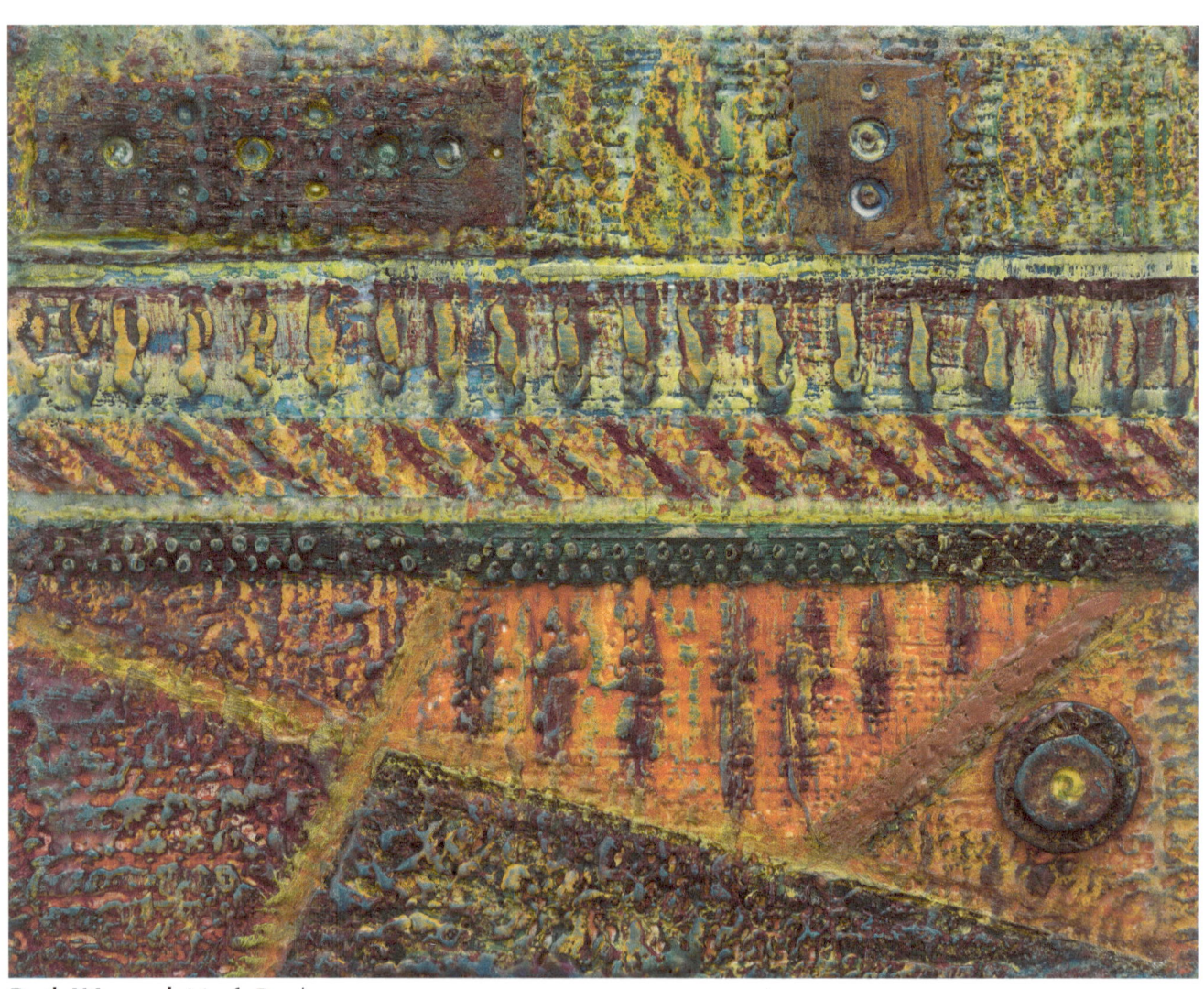

Ruth Warnock | Left Bank

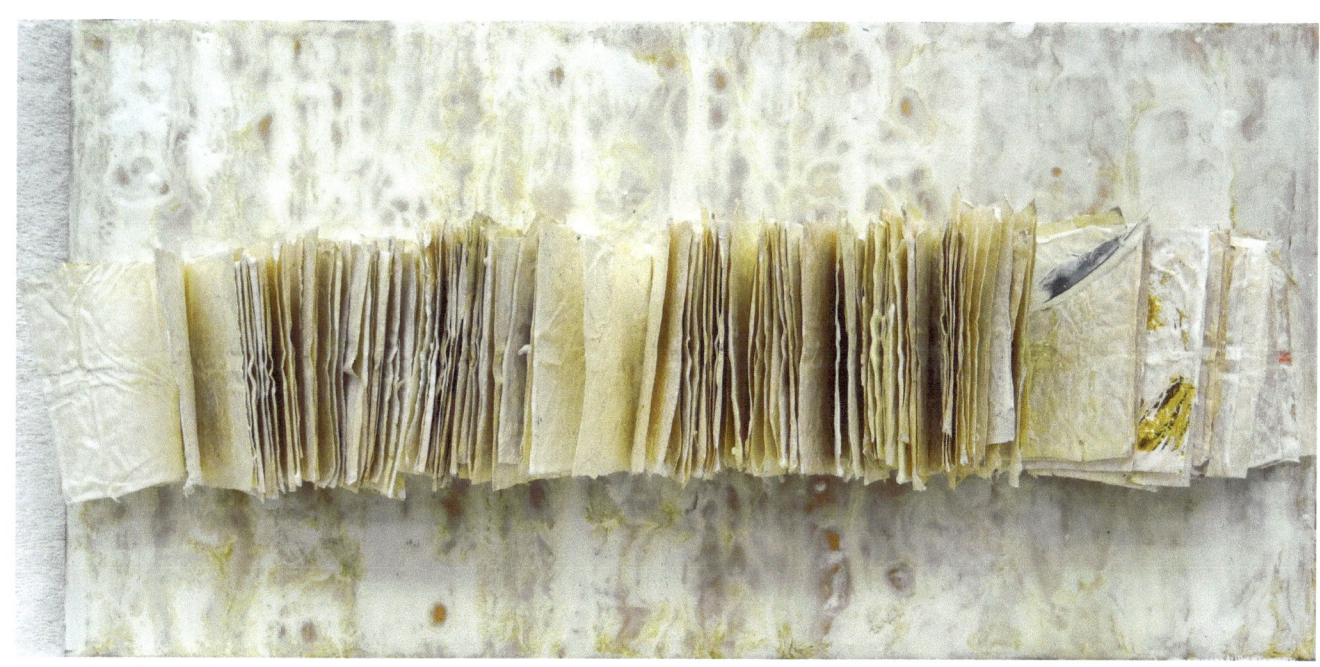

Kate Paul | Ledger

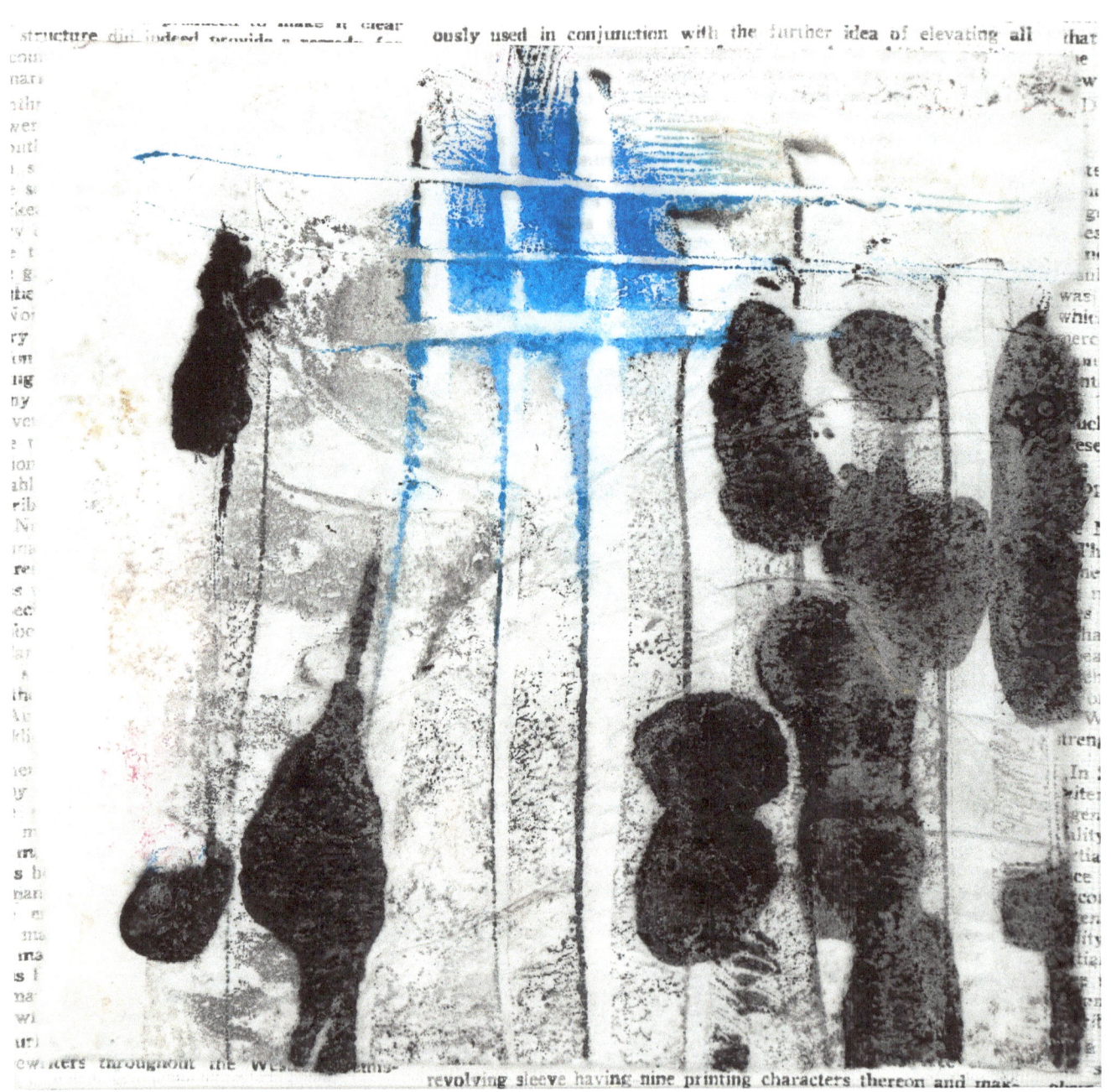

Rosemary Lee | On the Written Word

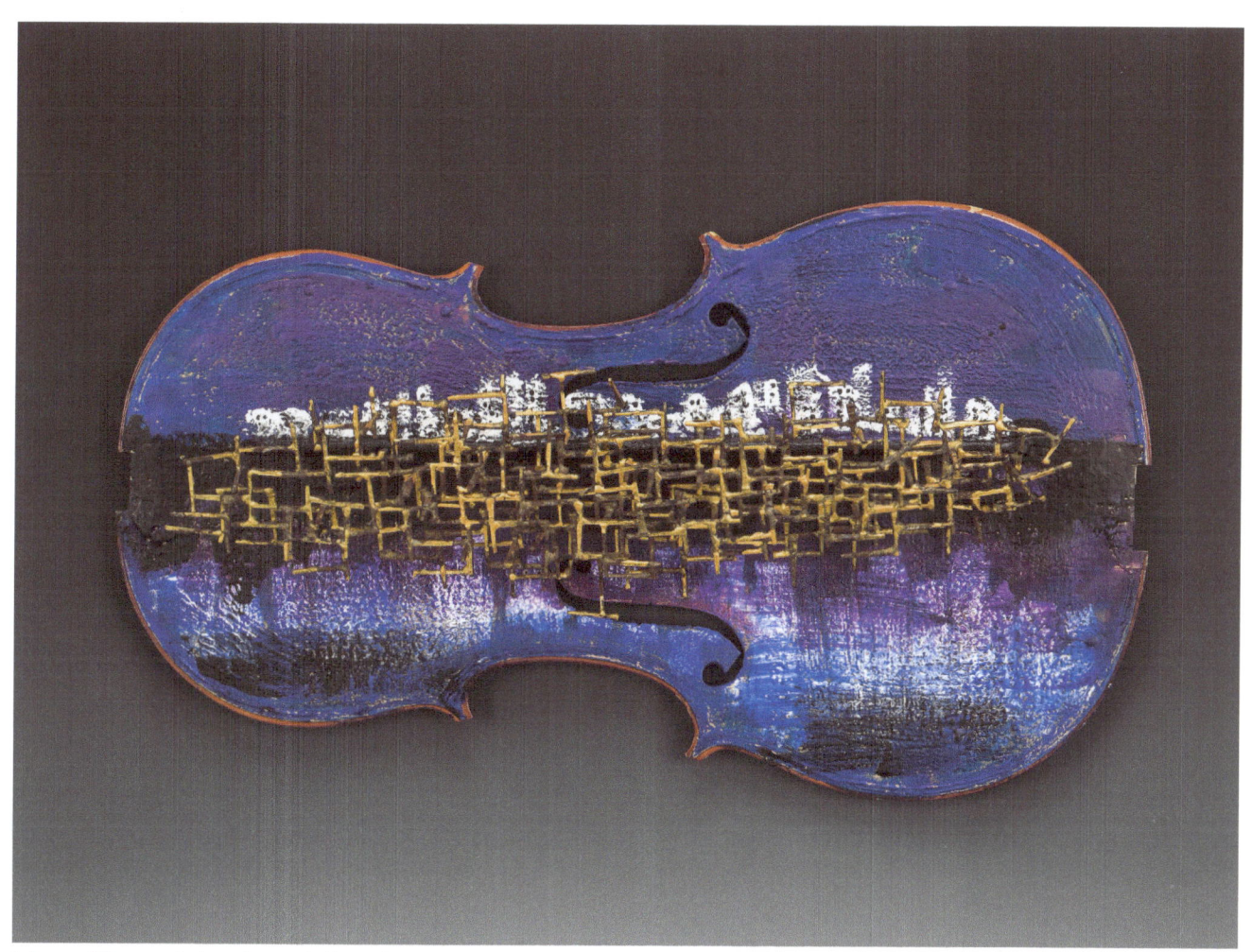

Nora Chapa Mendoza | City Scape

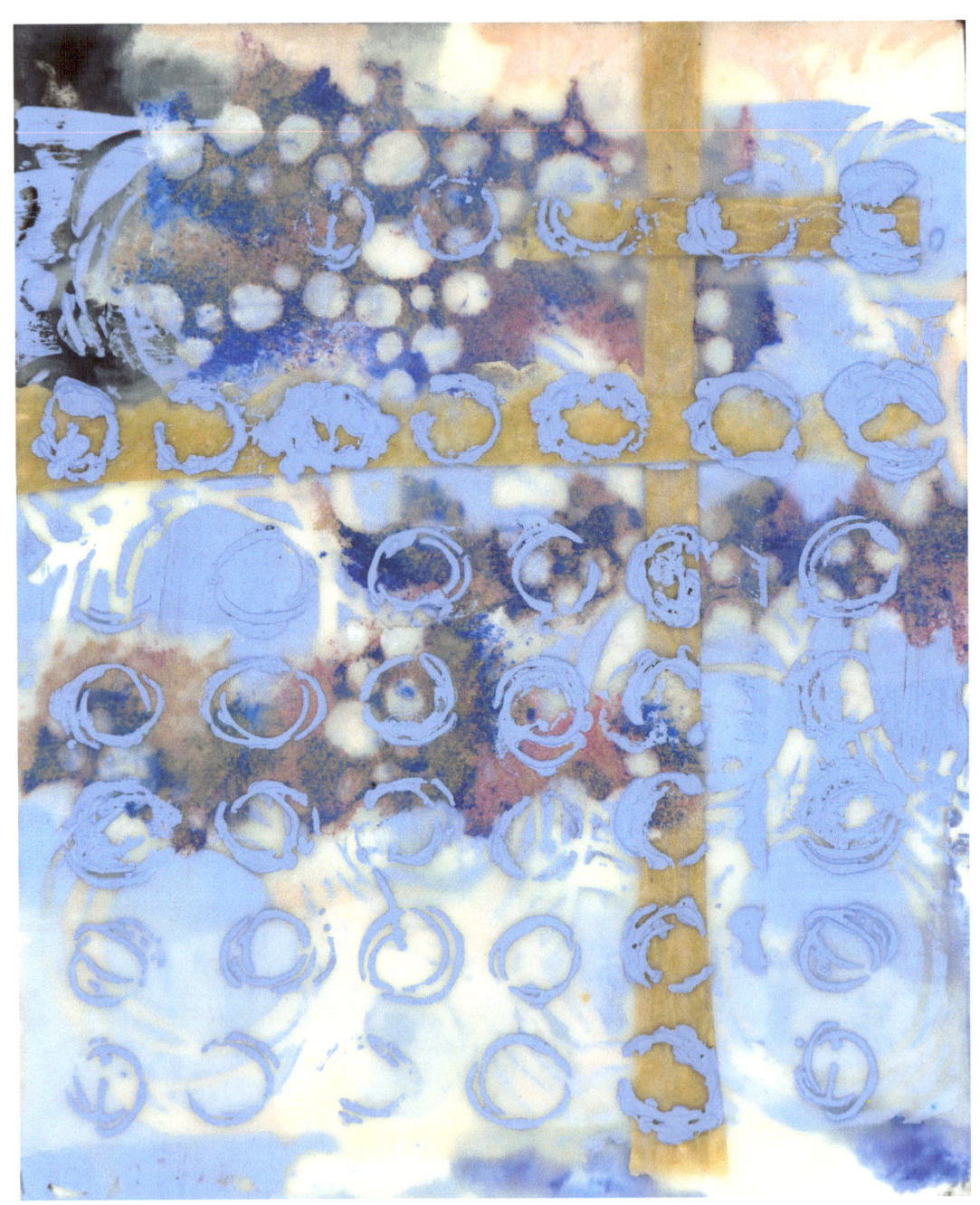

Martha Van Raaphorst | *Blue Heaven*

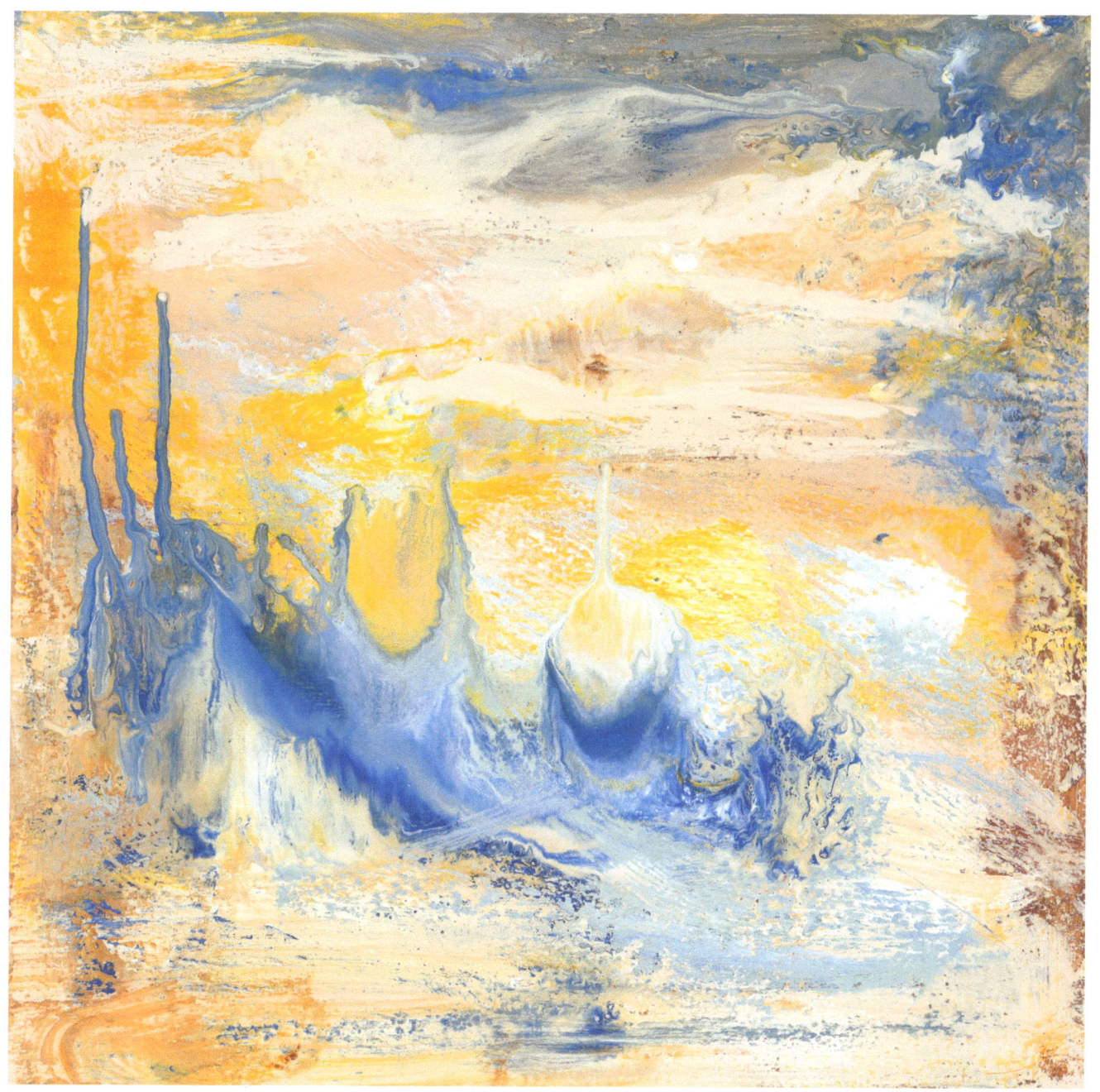

Edee Joppich | Blues Rising

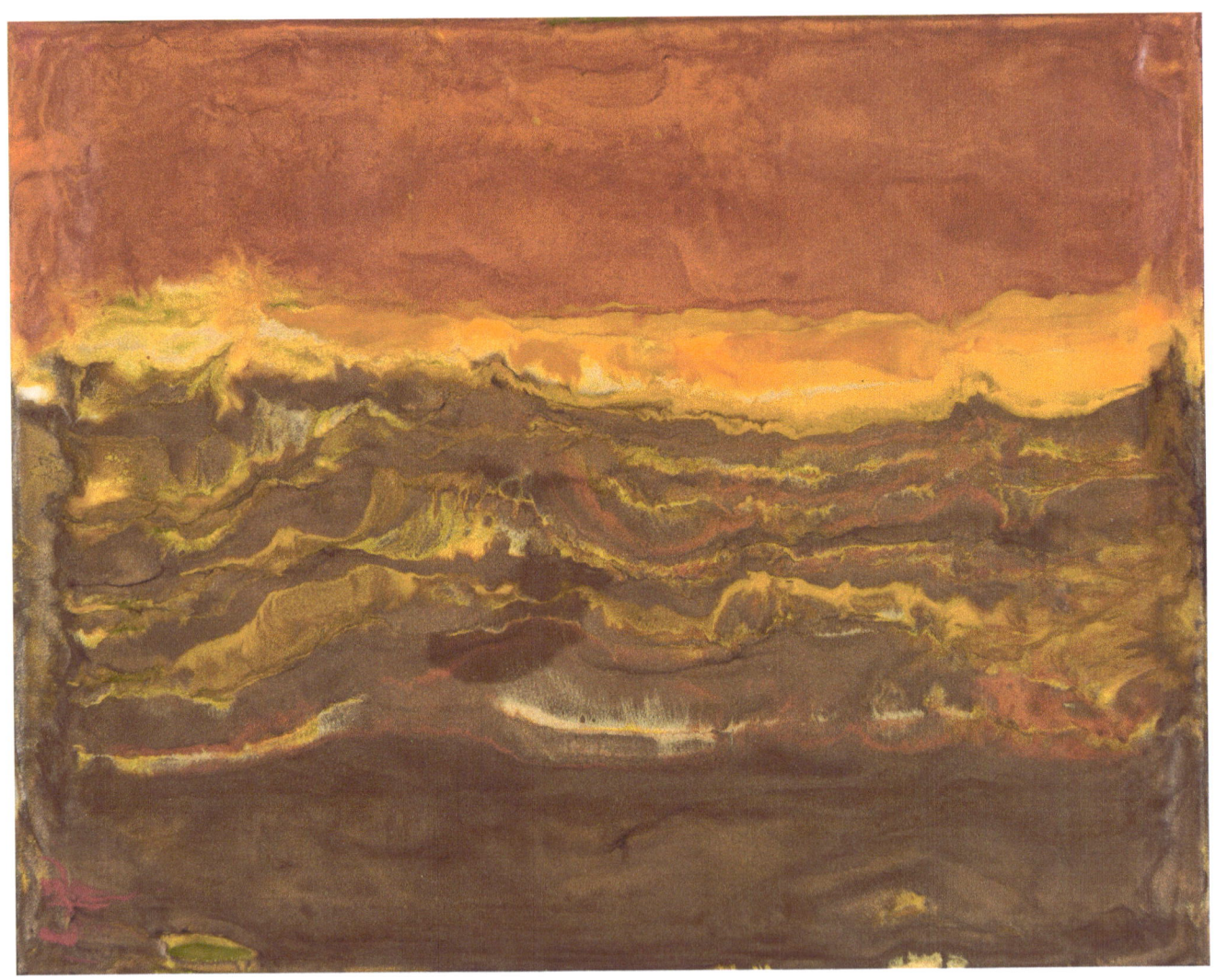

Gwen Downs | Copperscape

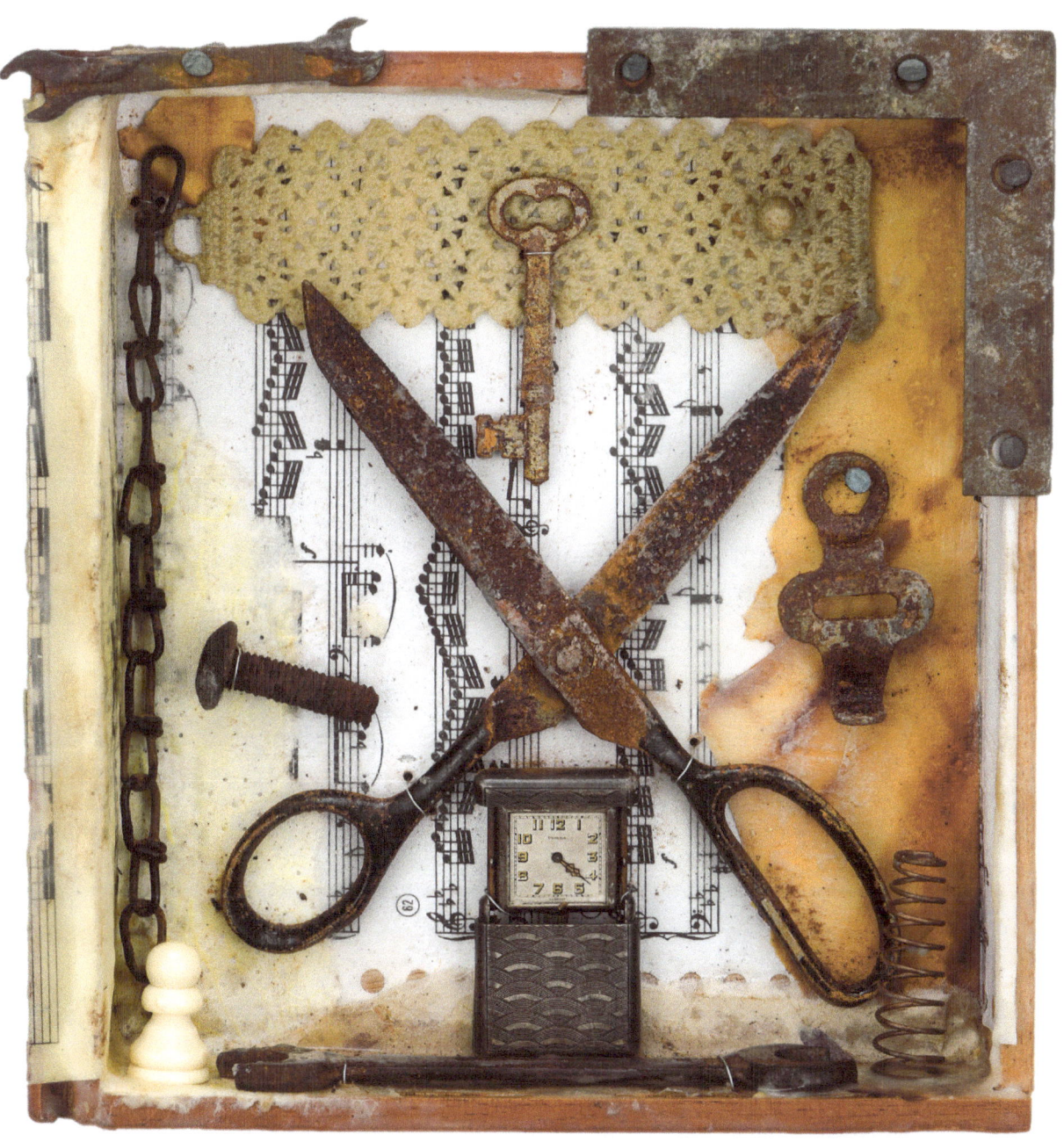

Ruth Warnock | Otherness

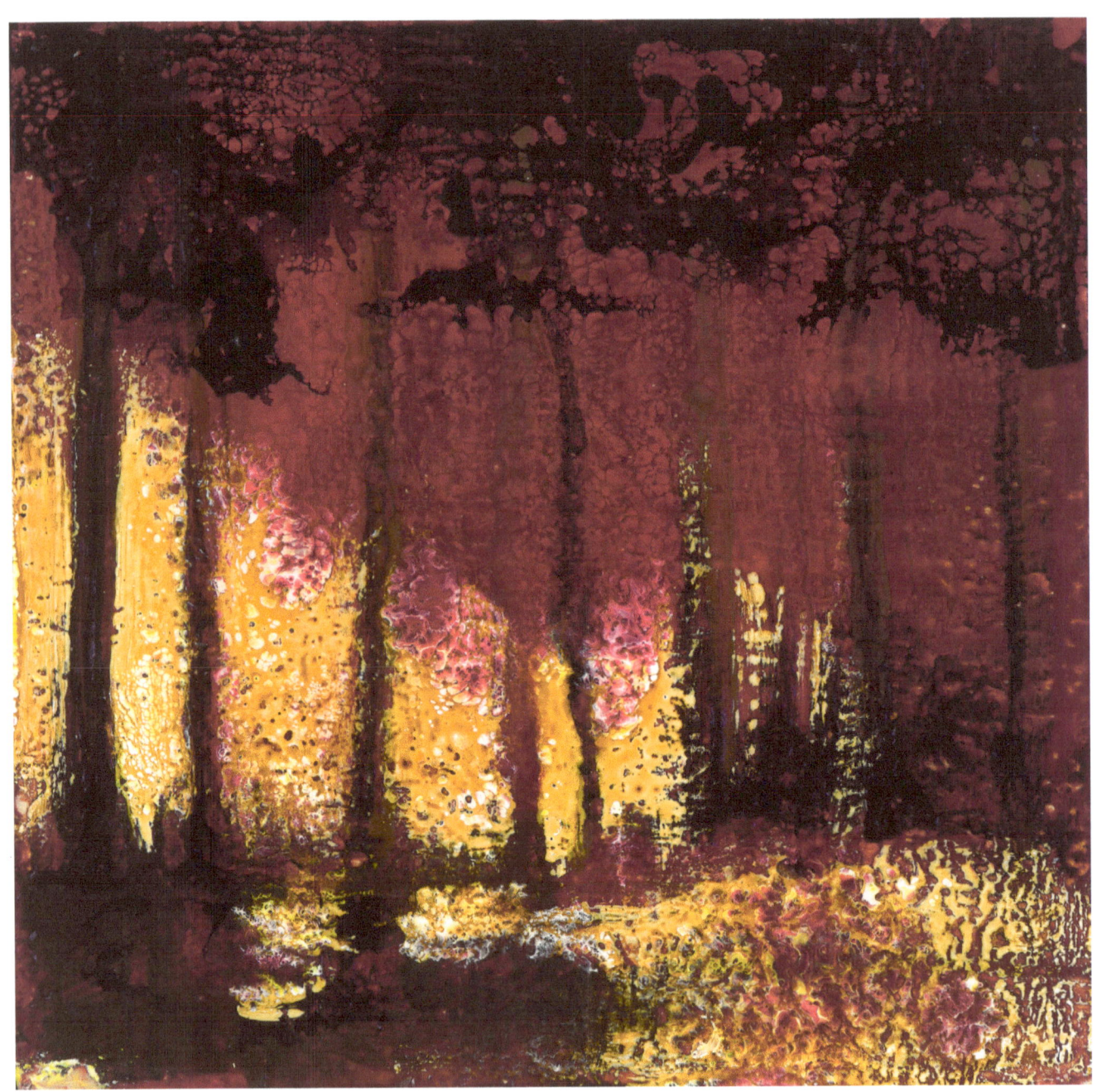

Kim Ensch | Dark Forest

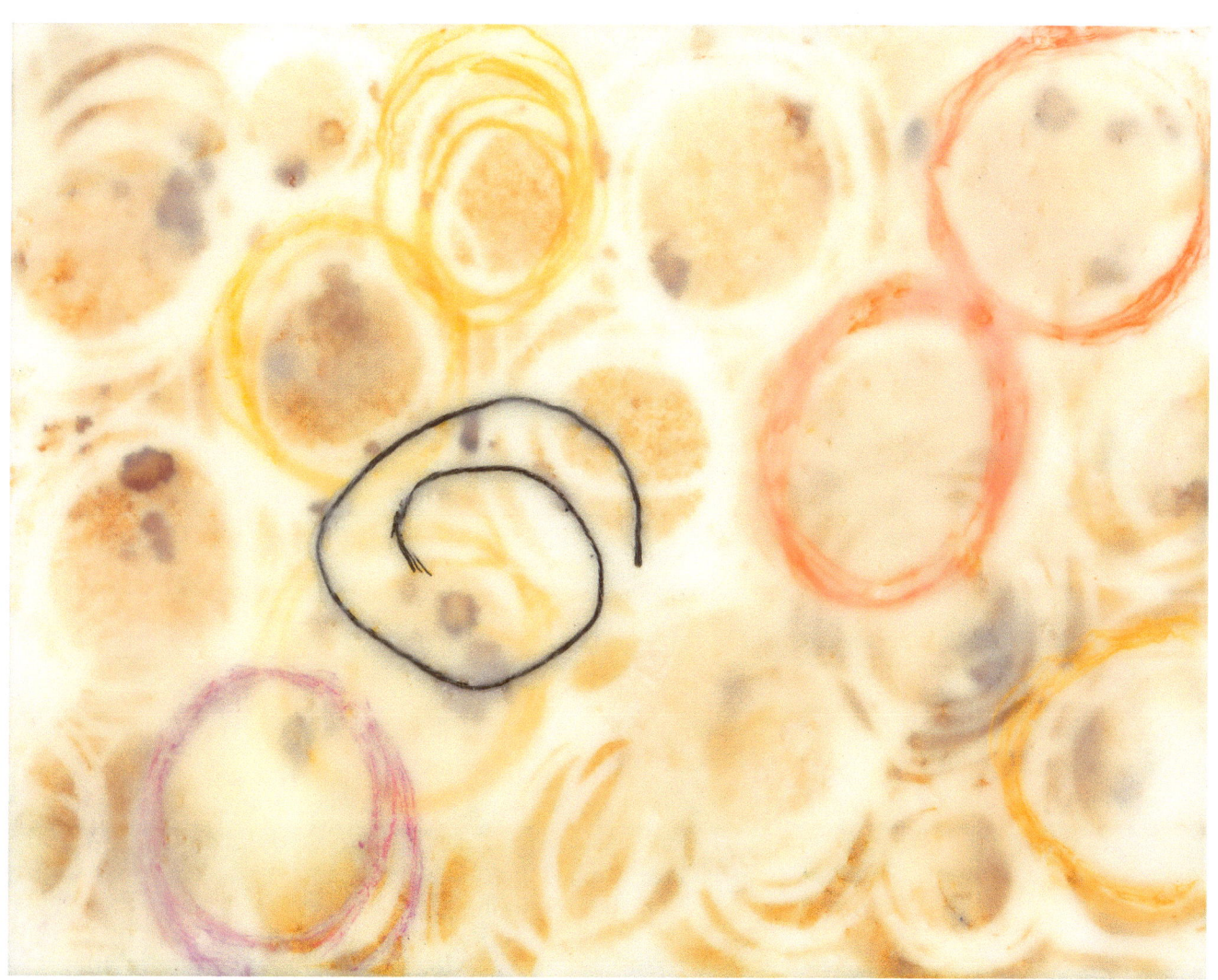

Candace Law | Hide in Plain Sight

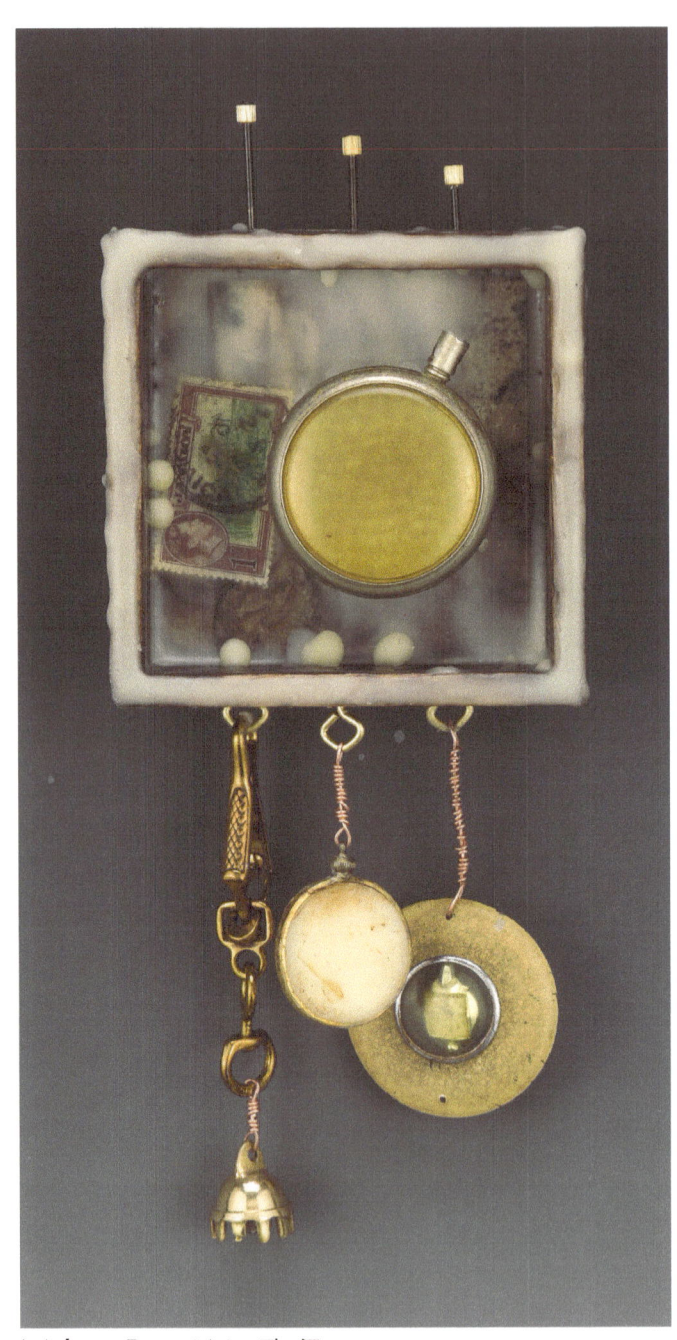

Melissa Rian | No Fly Zone

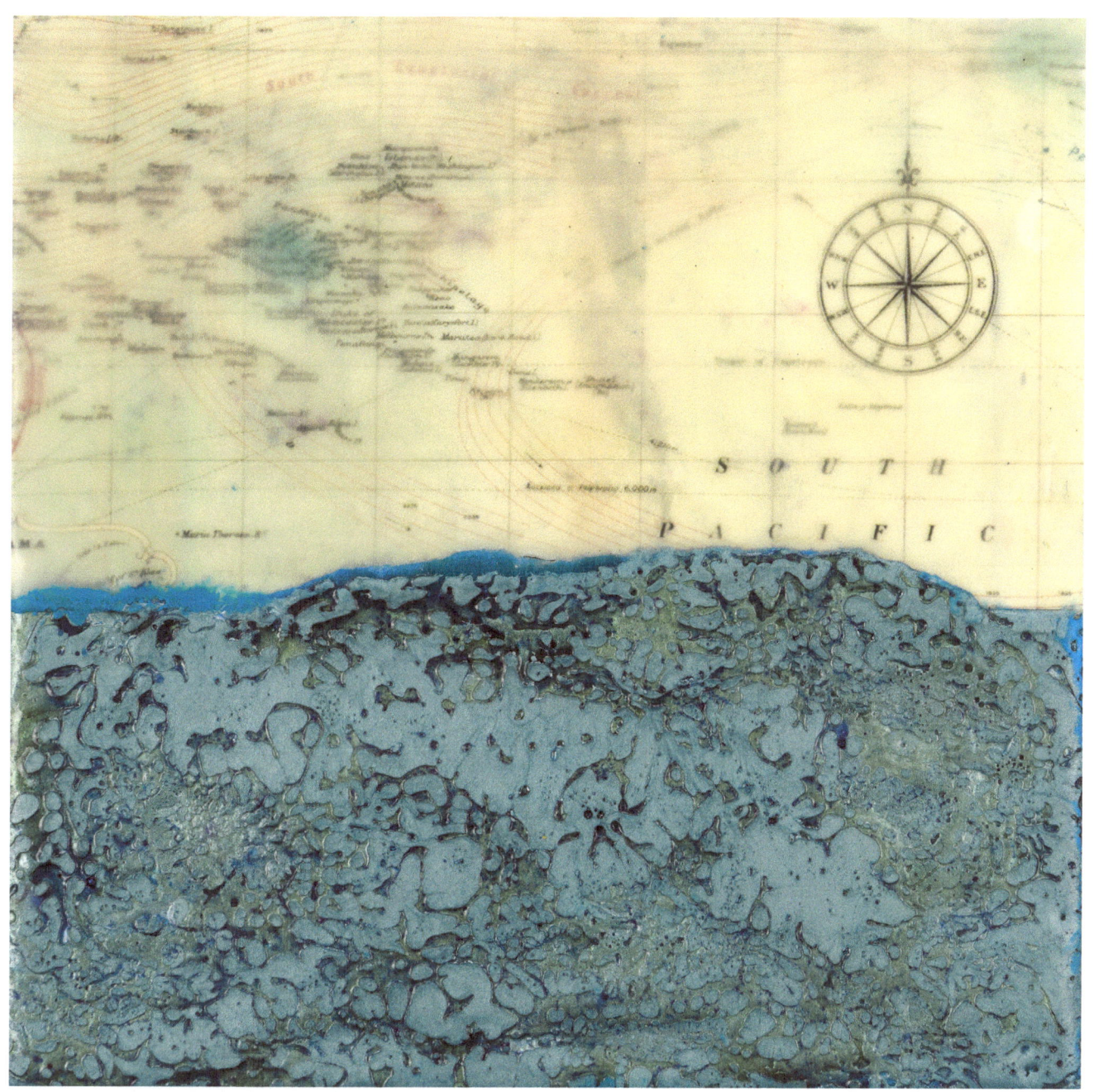

Wendy Wernet | Ocean

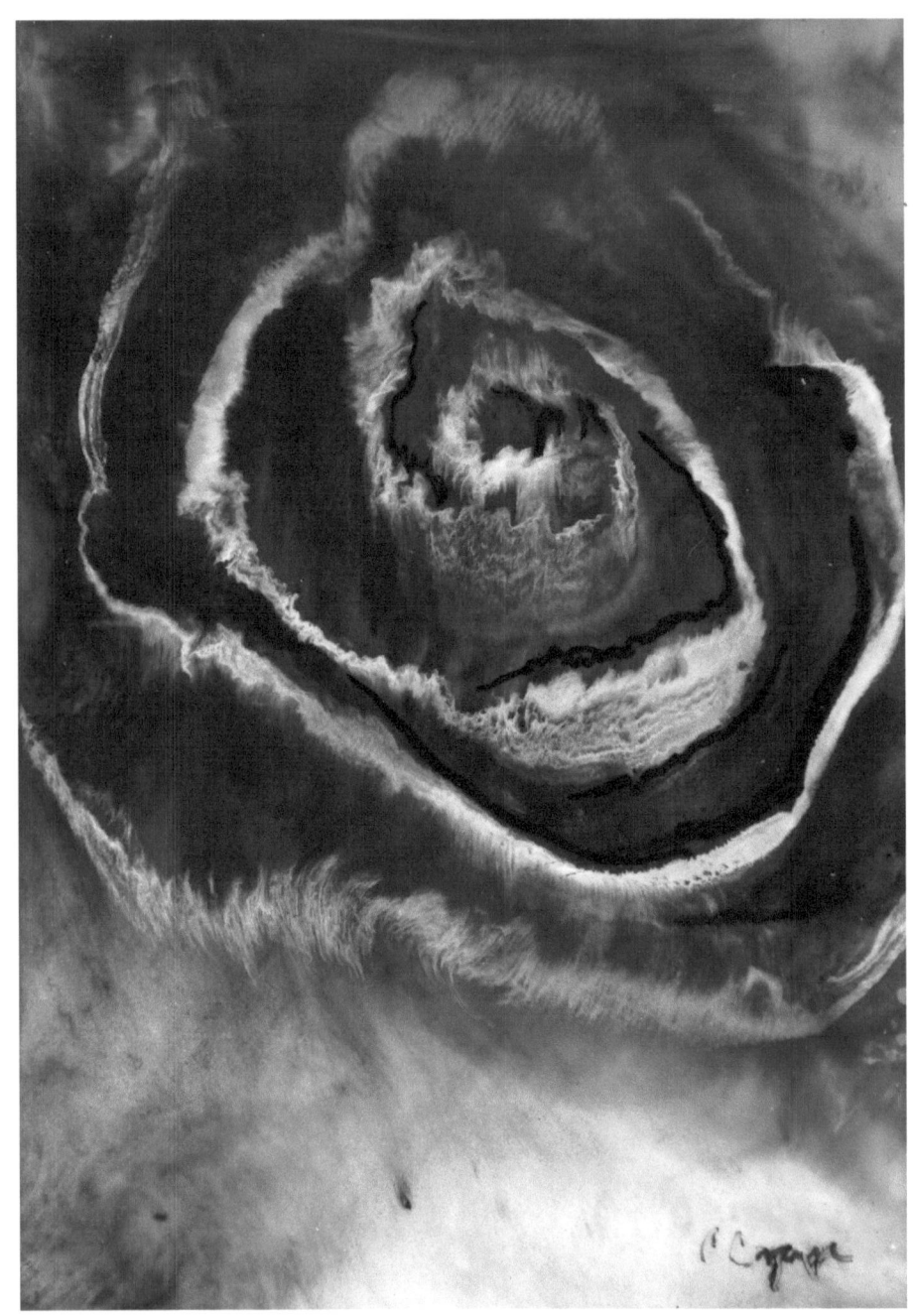

Christina Czaja | My Black Abyss

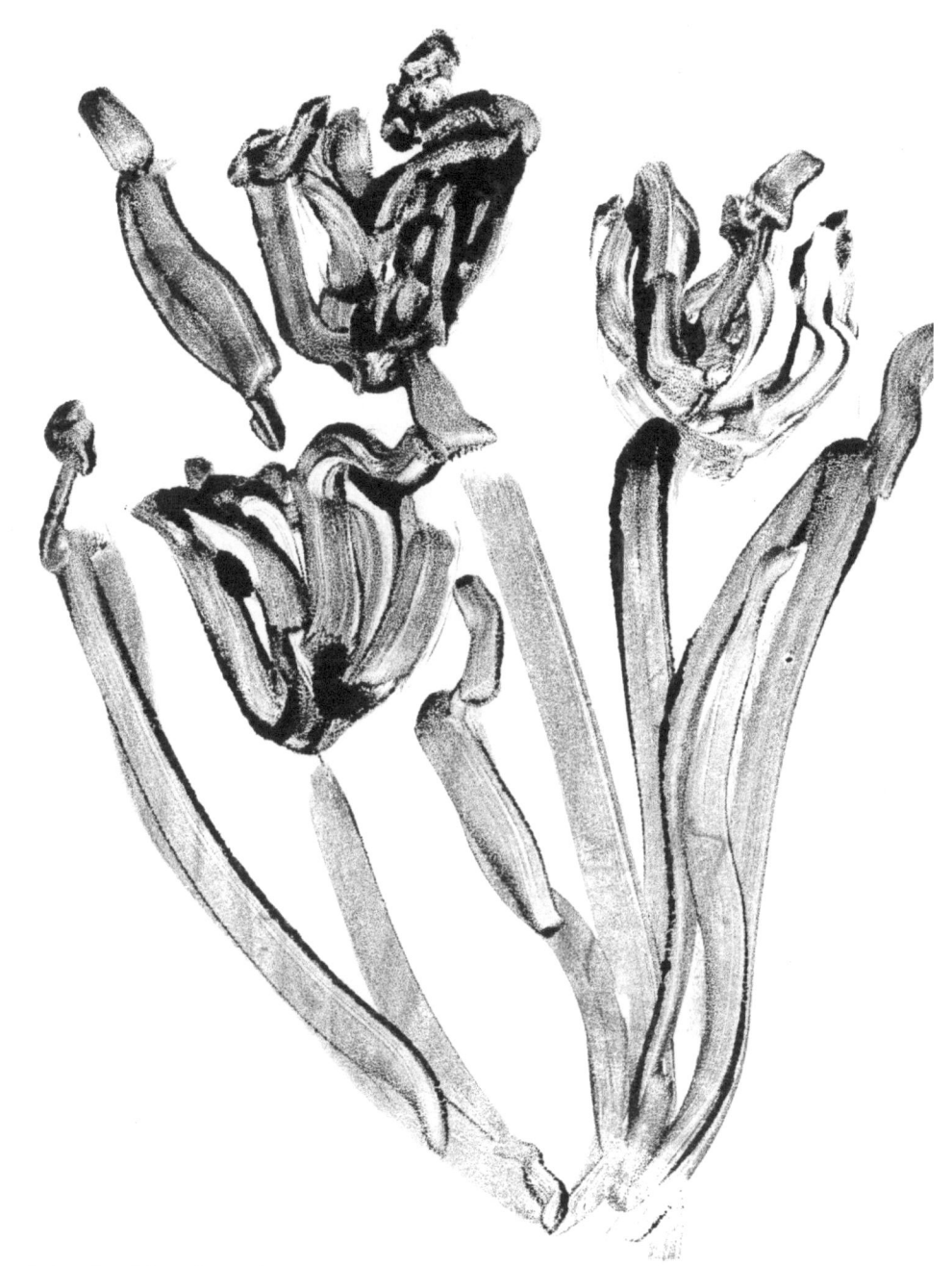

Martha Van Raaphorst | Once upon a Spring

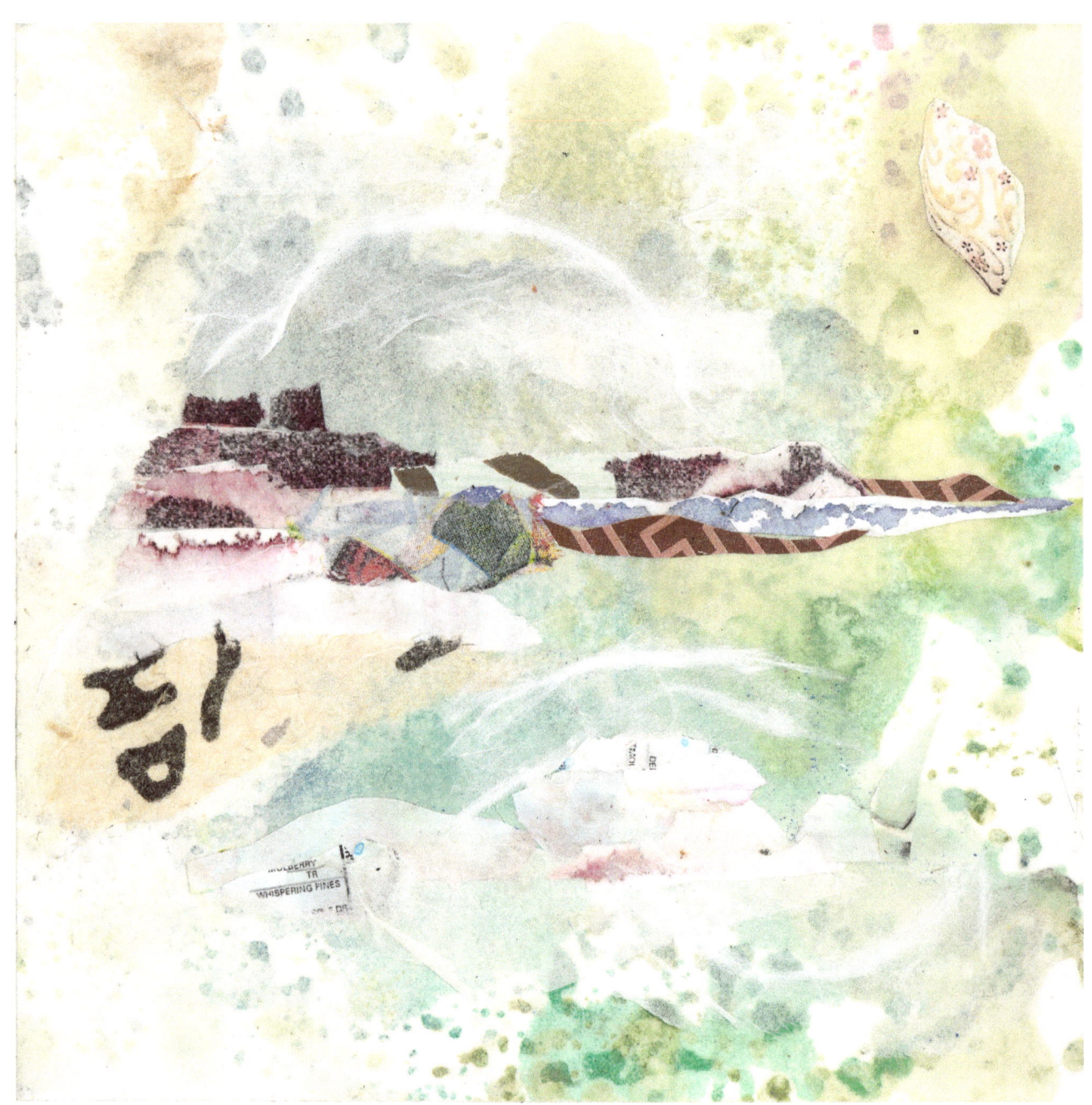

Janice Key | Landscape 1

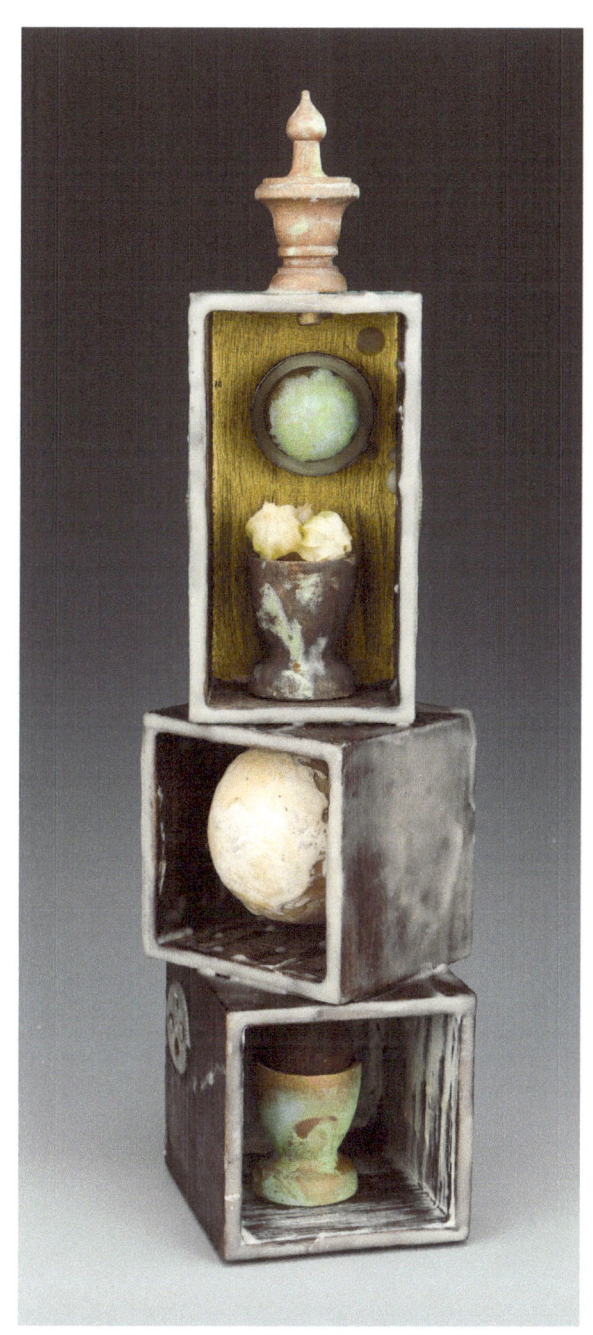

Melissa Rian | The Egg Came First

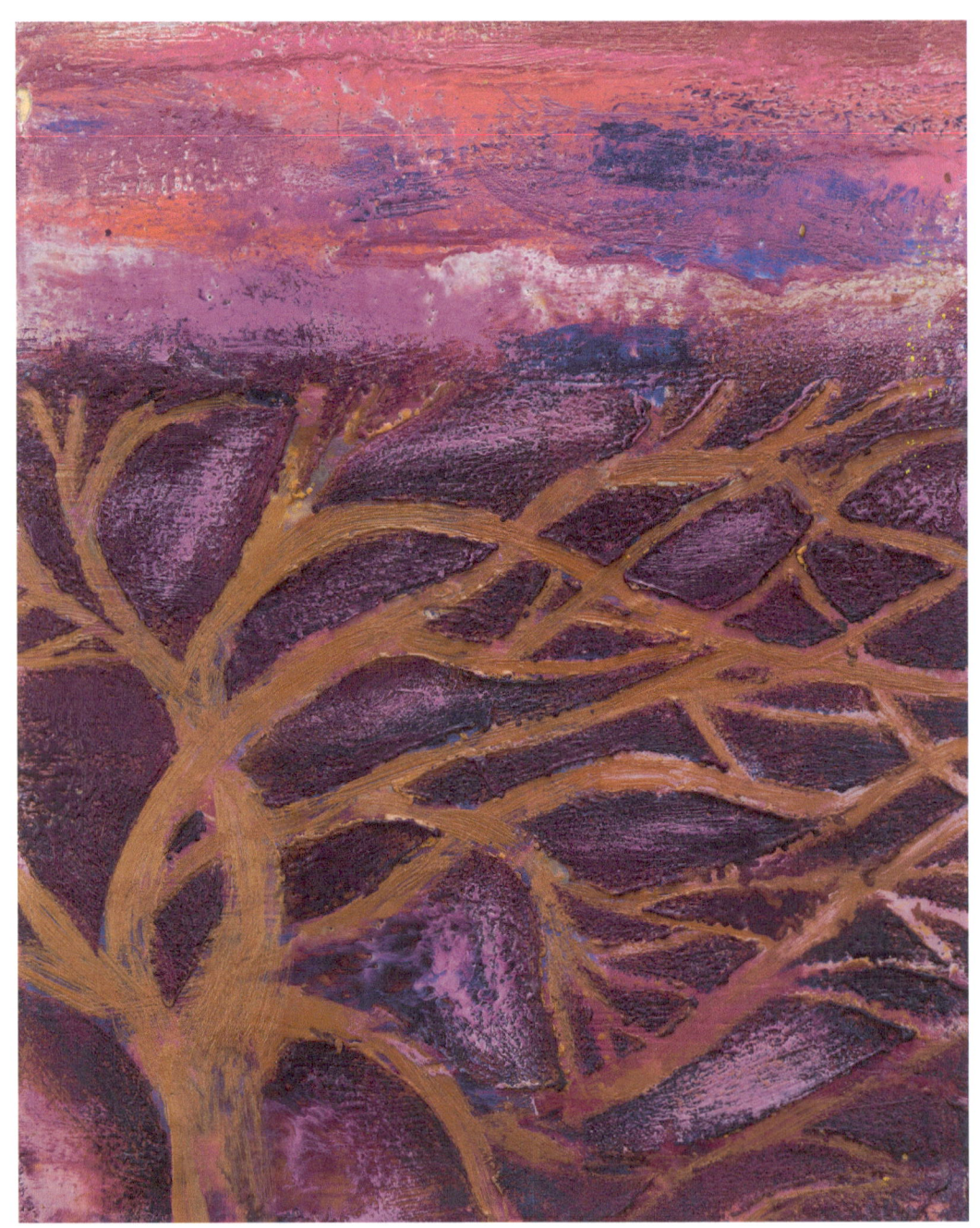

Suzanne Allen | Blowing Branches

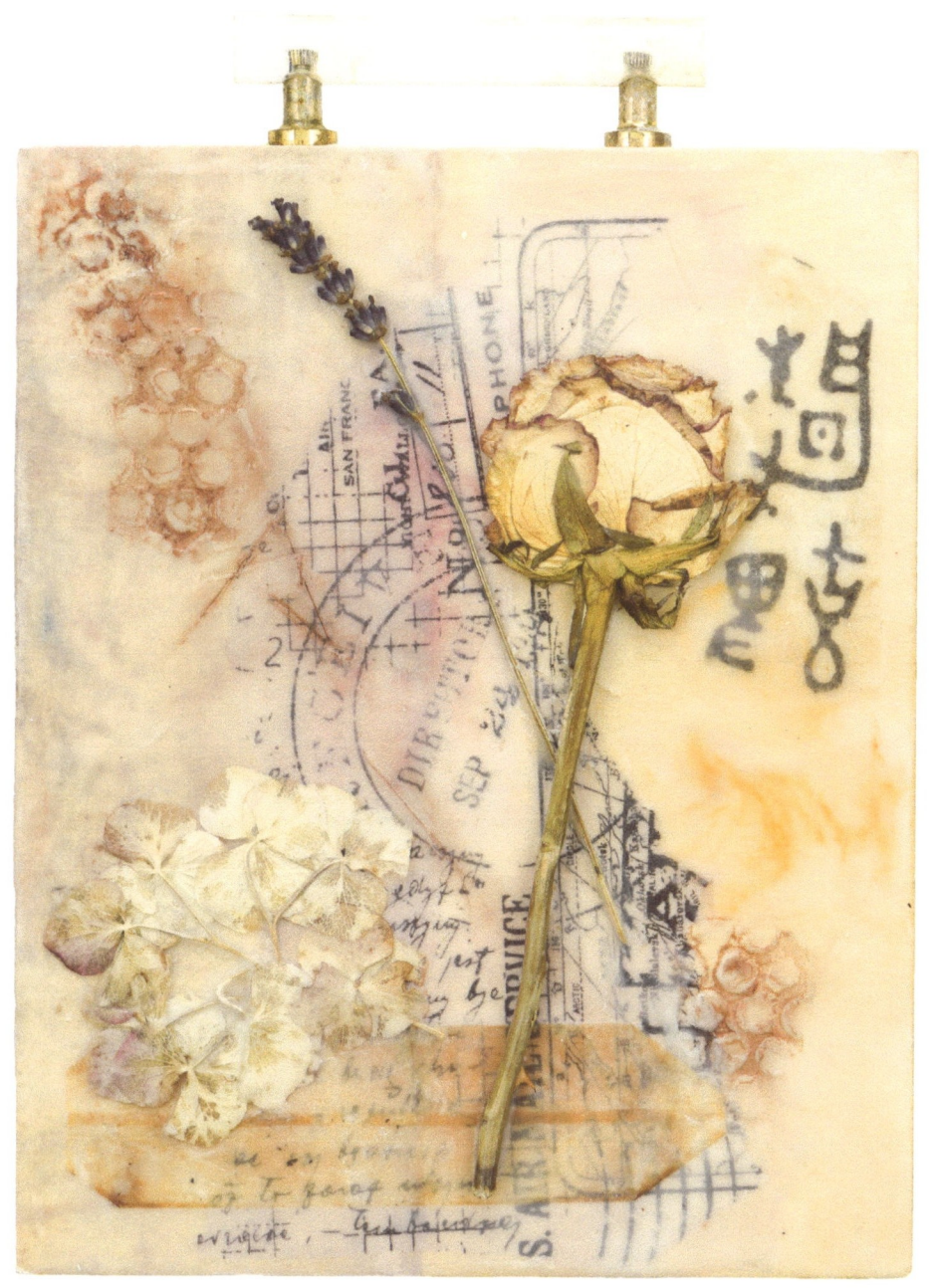

Kathy Jacobi | Last Summer

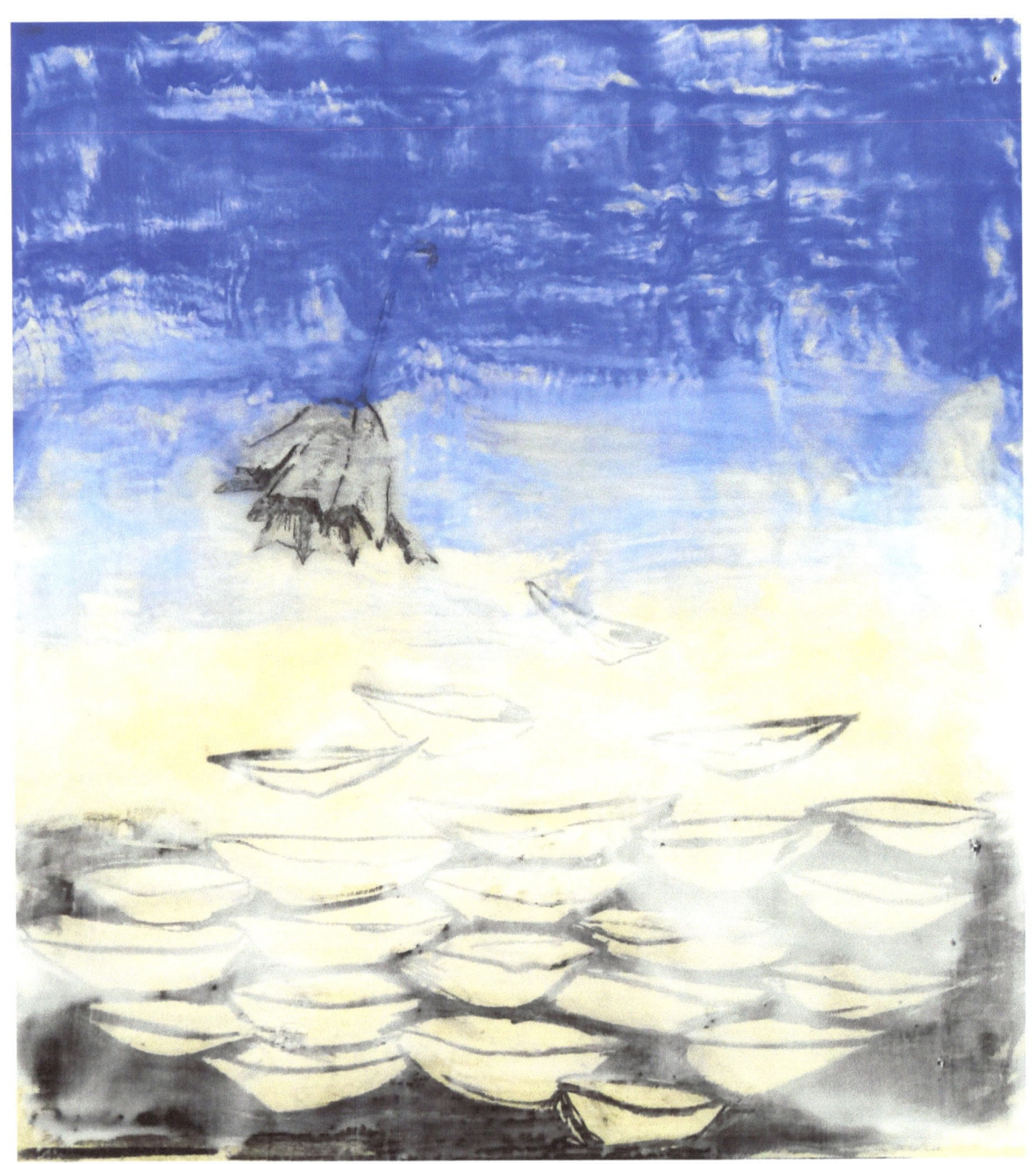

Kate Paul | *Storm Rise*

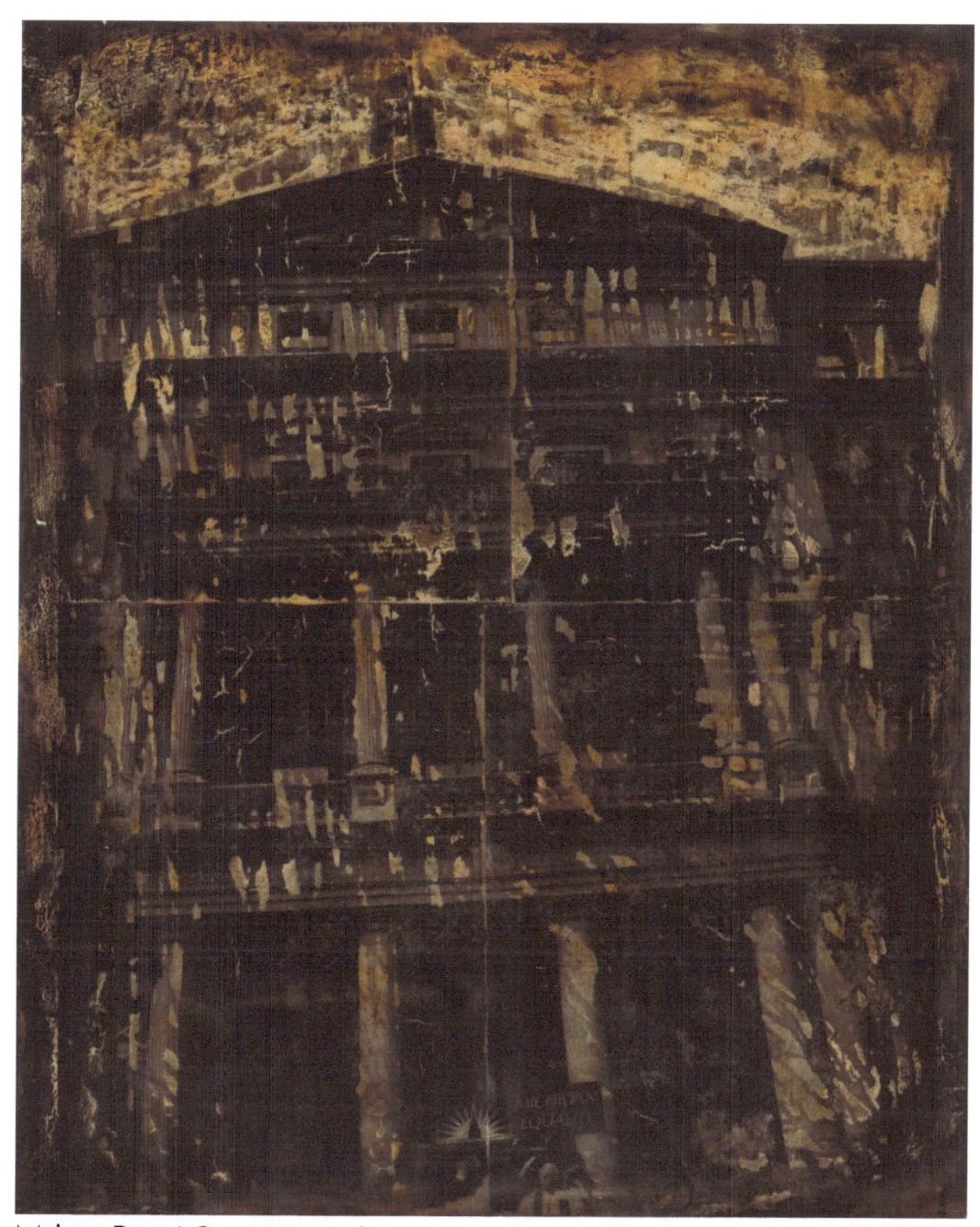

Melissa Rian | Commitment Ceremony

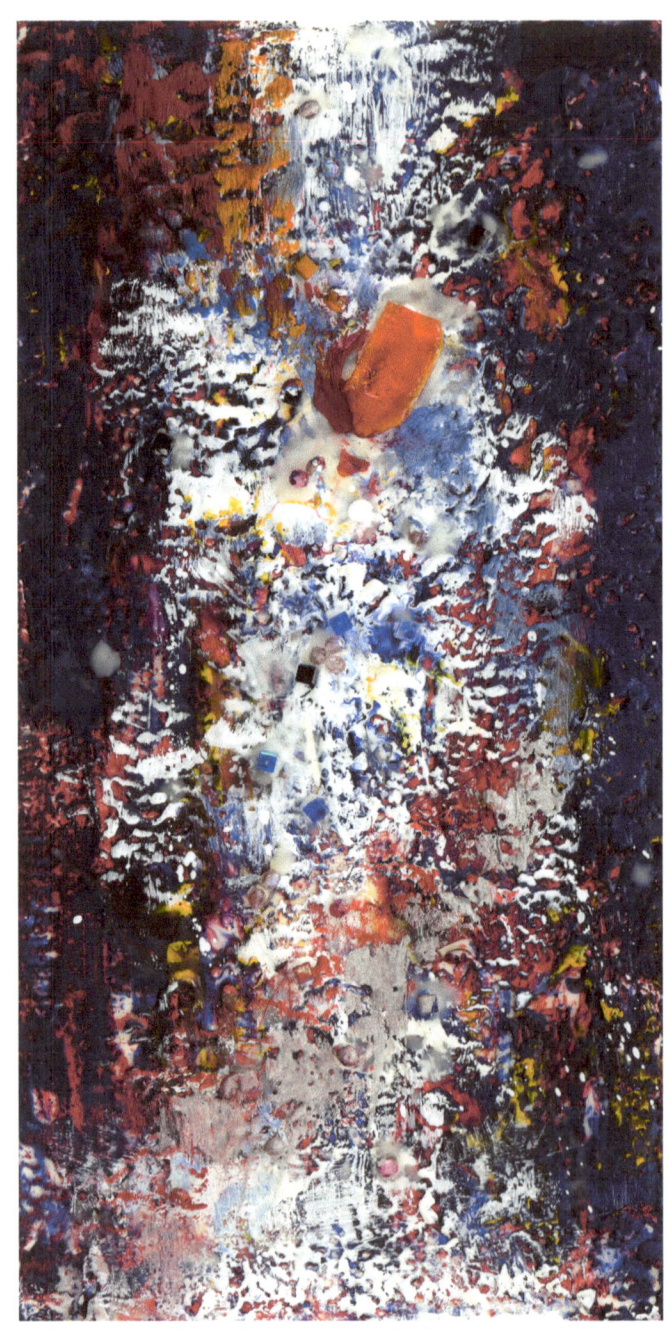

Edee Joppich | *Where Love Abides*

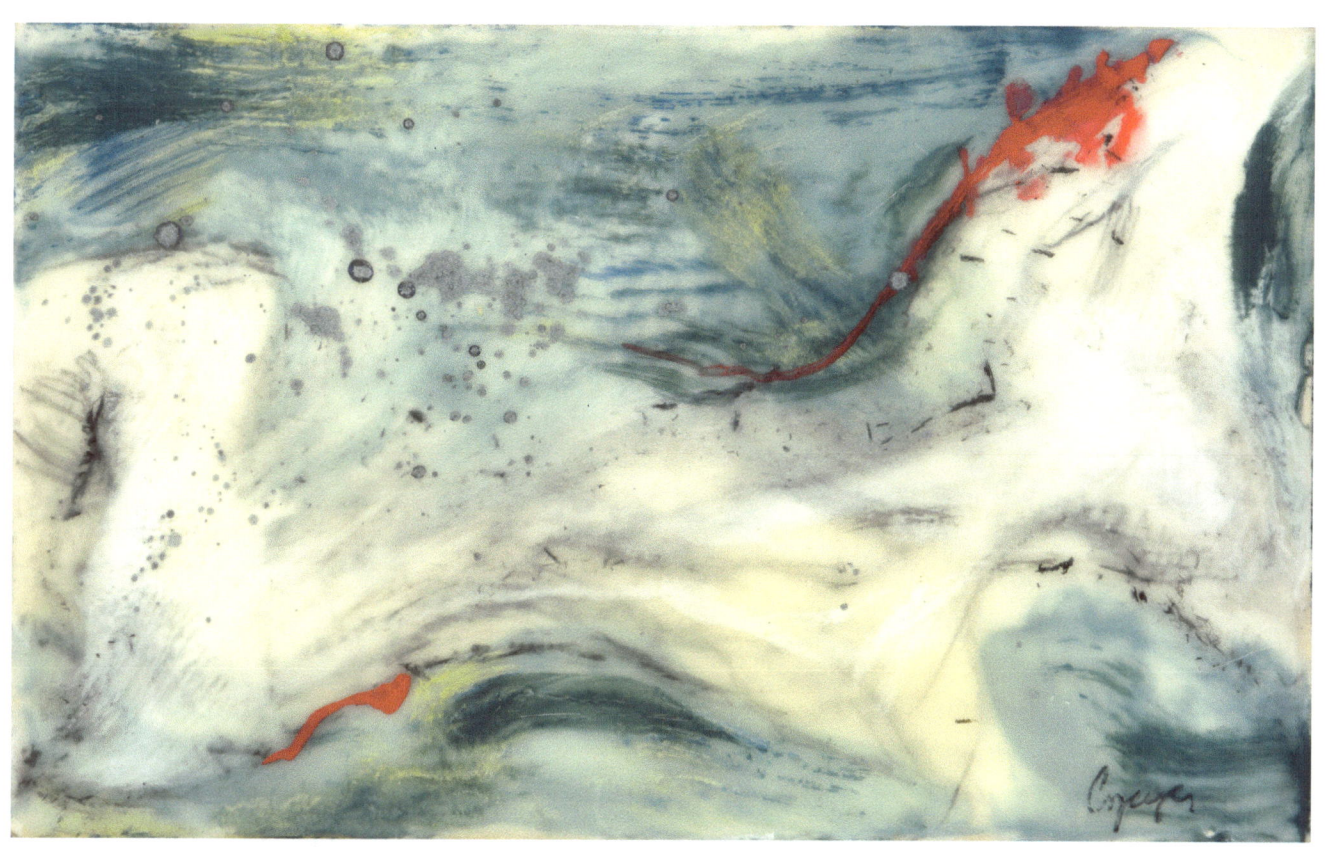

Christina Czaja | Blue Figure

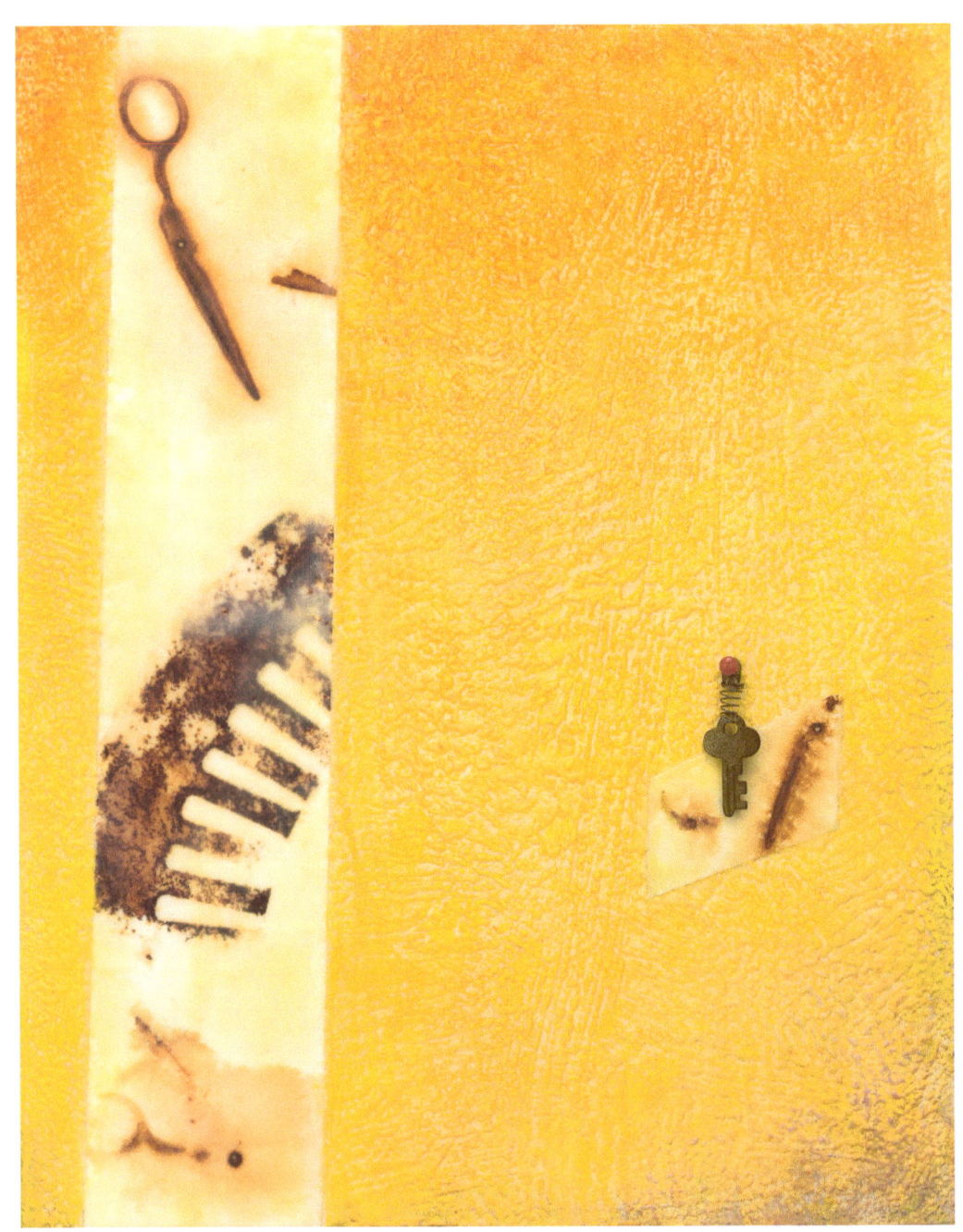

Candace Law | Unlock

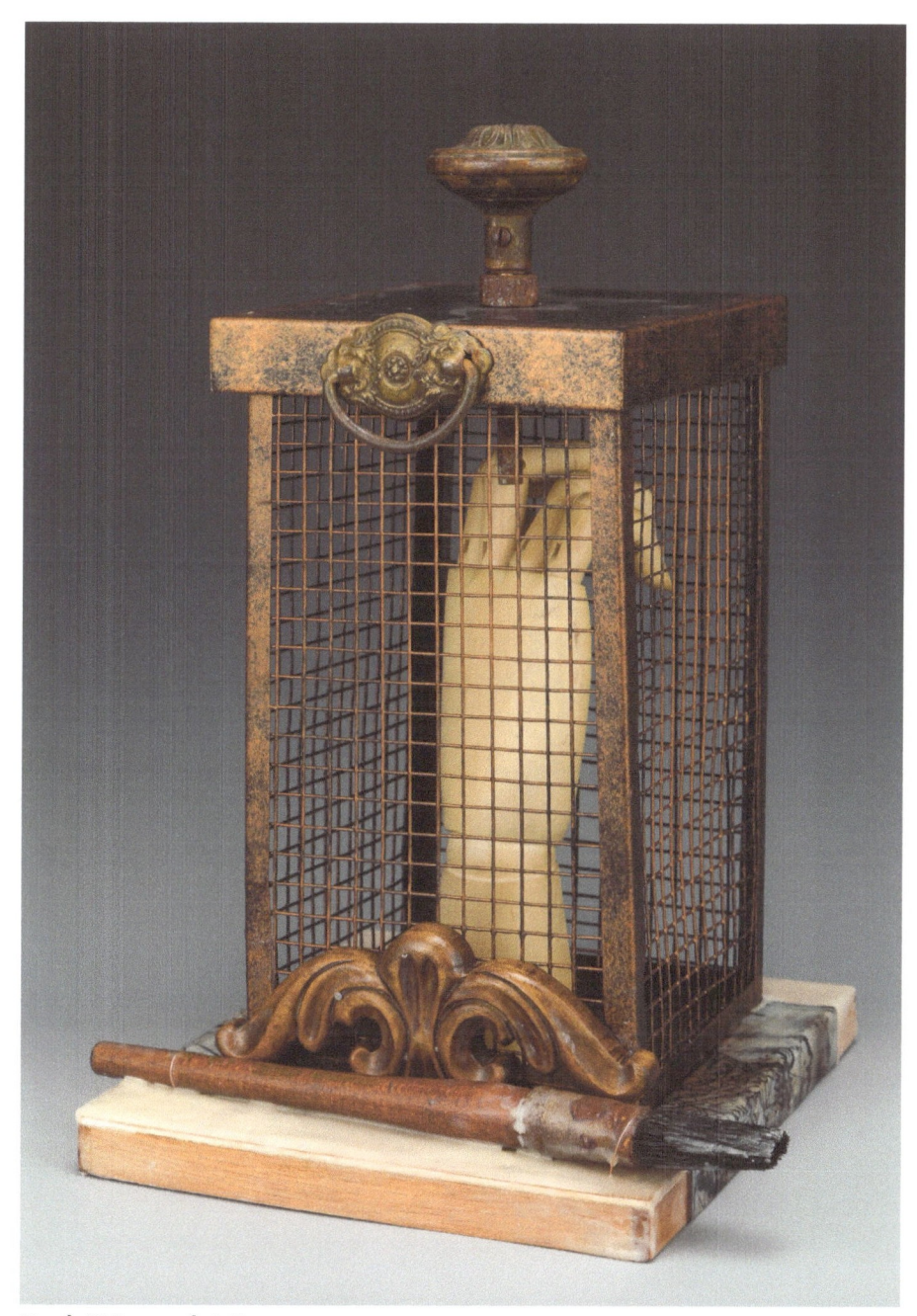

Ruth Warnock | Pentimento

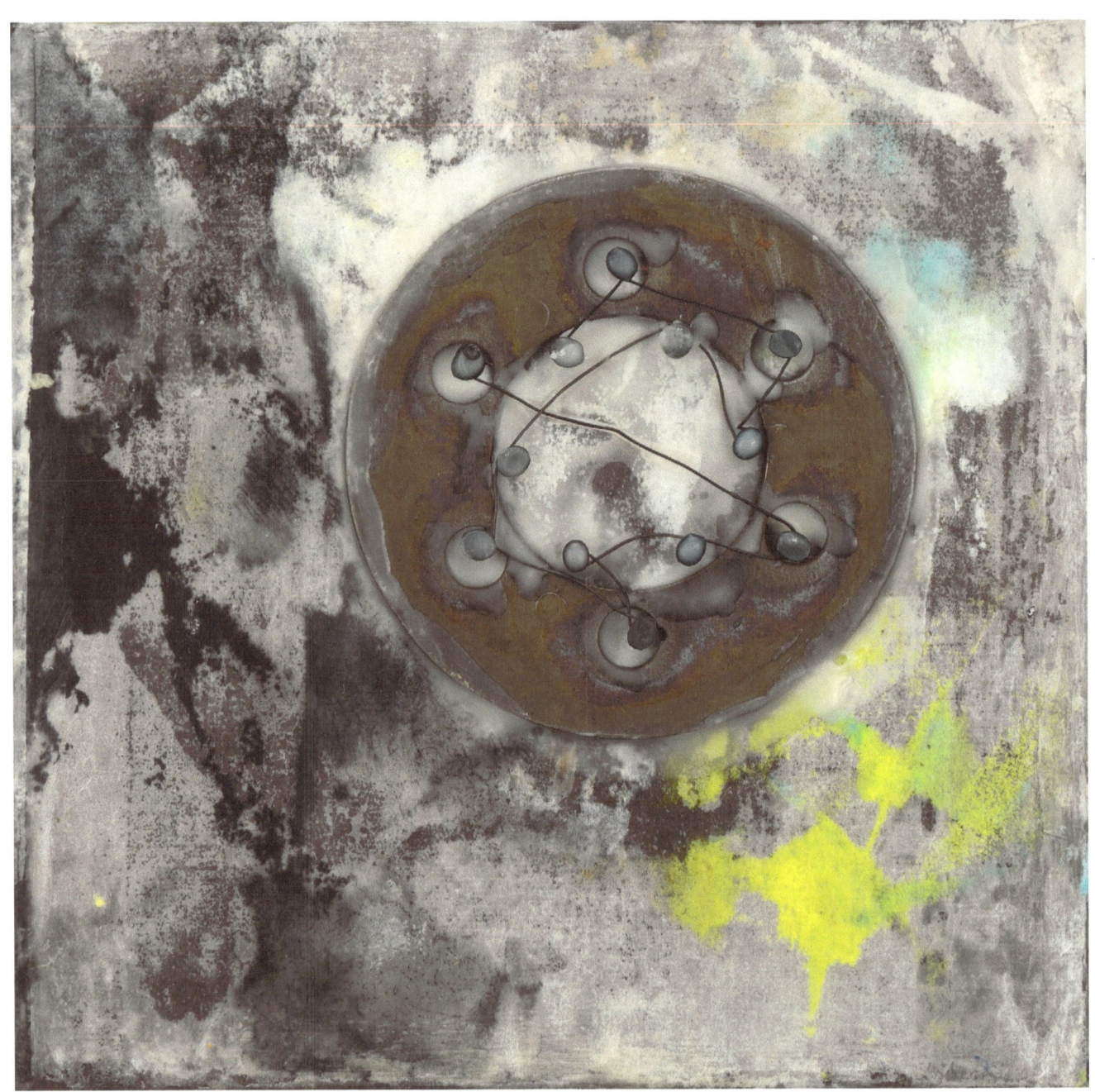

Kim Ensch | Grey Gear

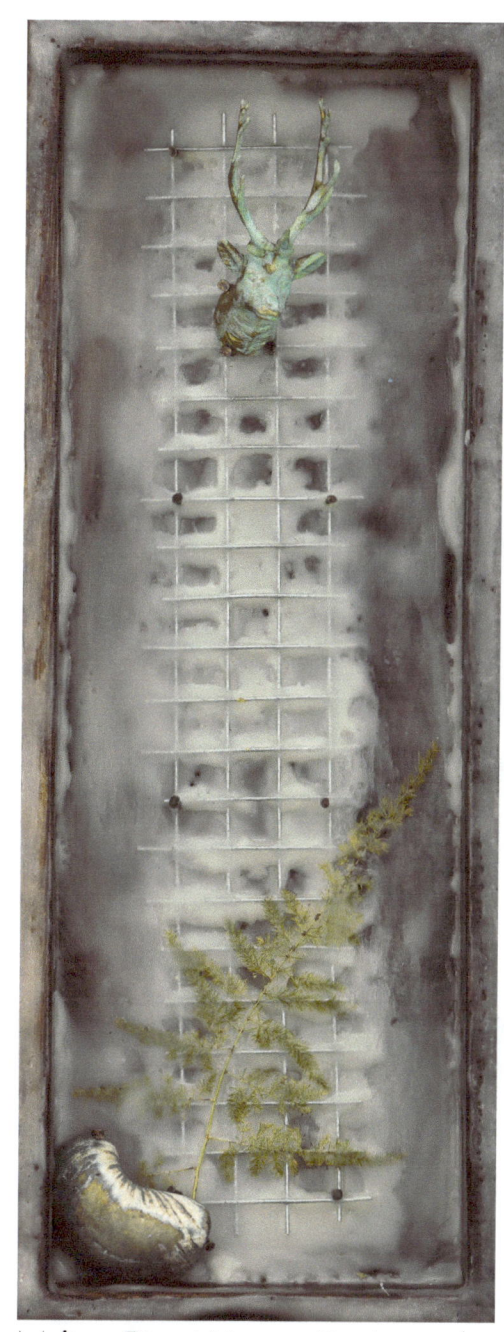

Melissa Rian | Natures Trophy

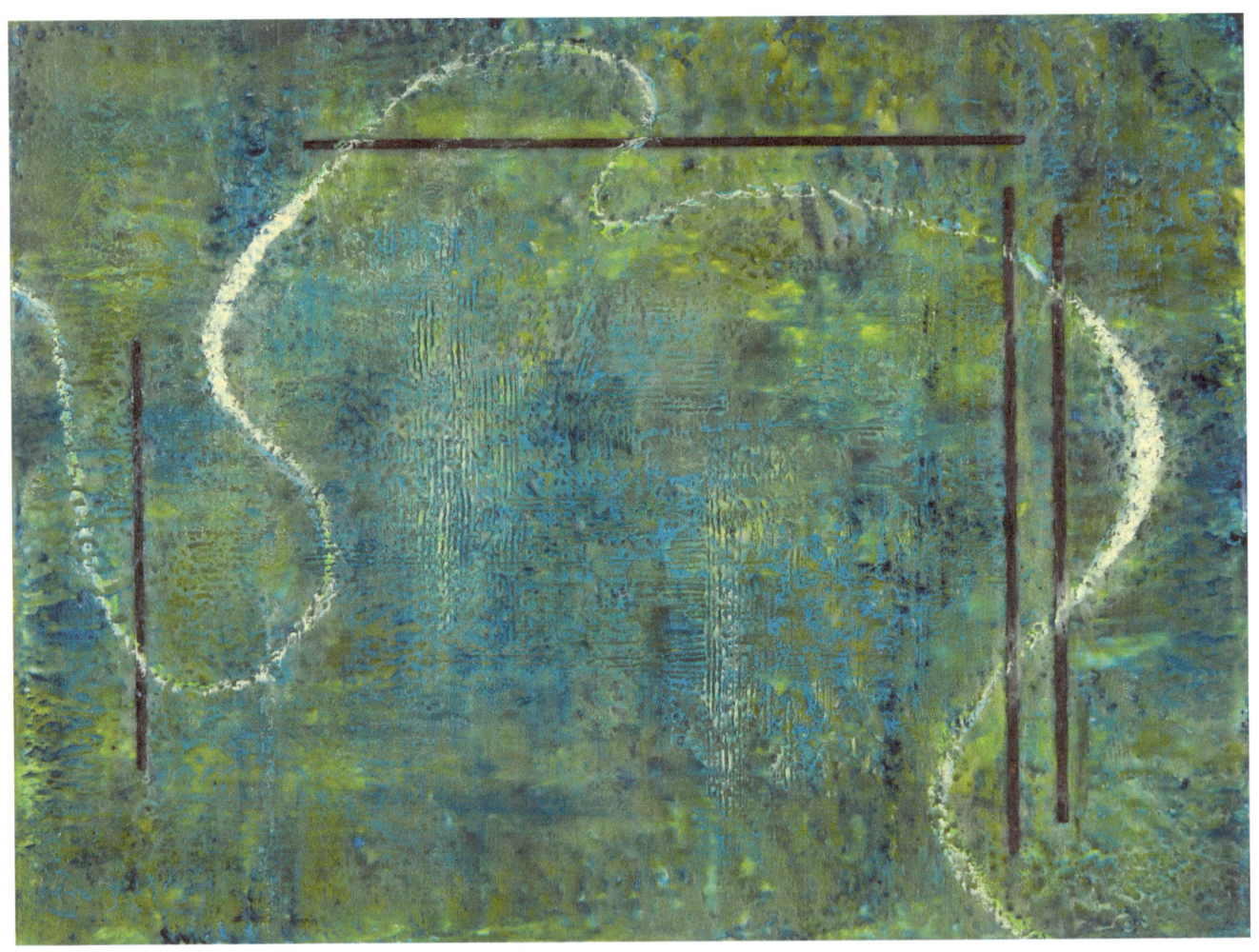

Candace Law | Wanderings

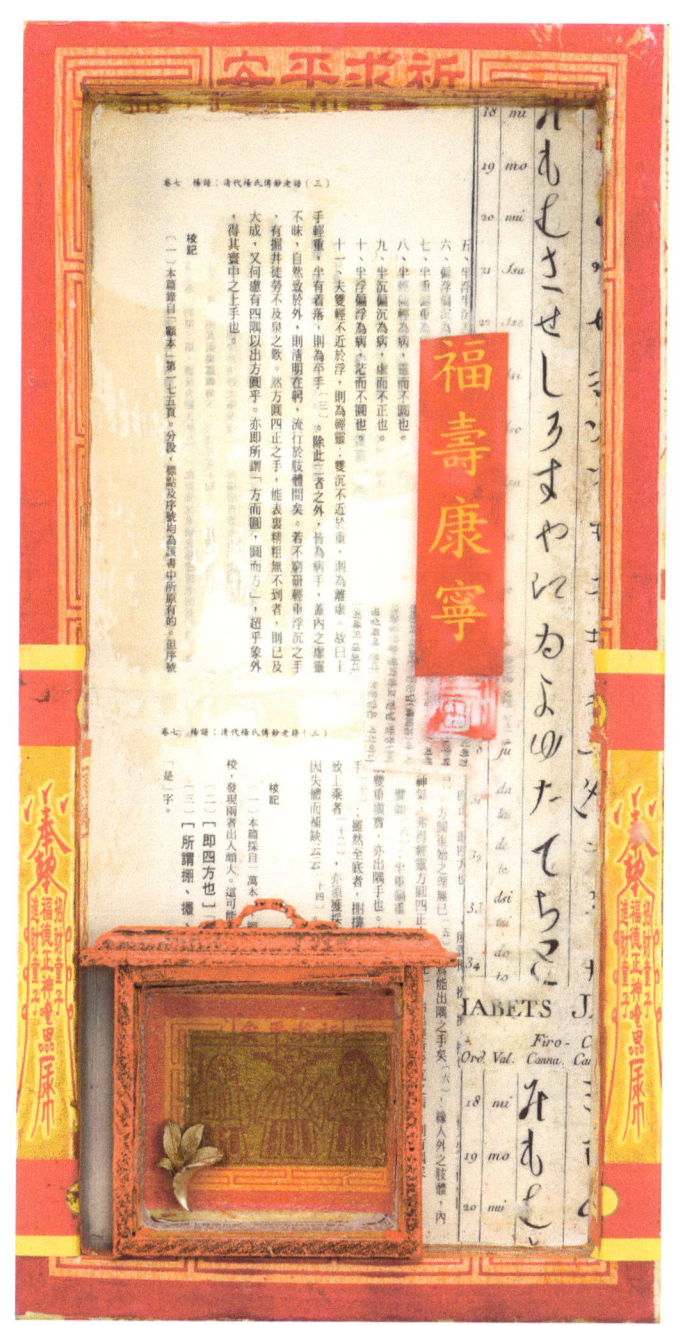

Suzanne Allen | Chopstick Temple

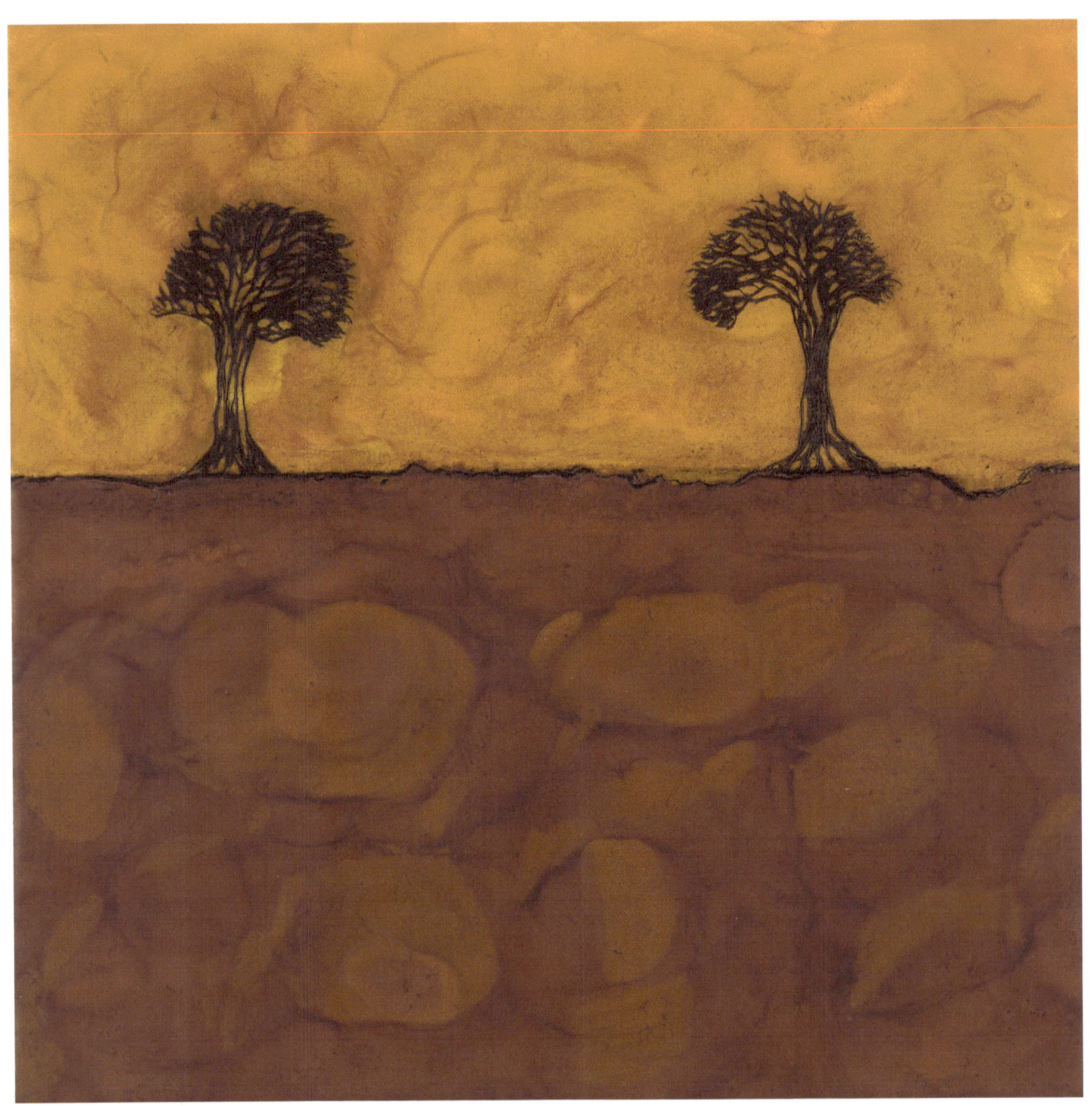

Wendy Wernet | Two Trees

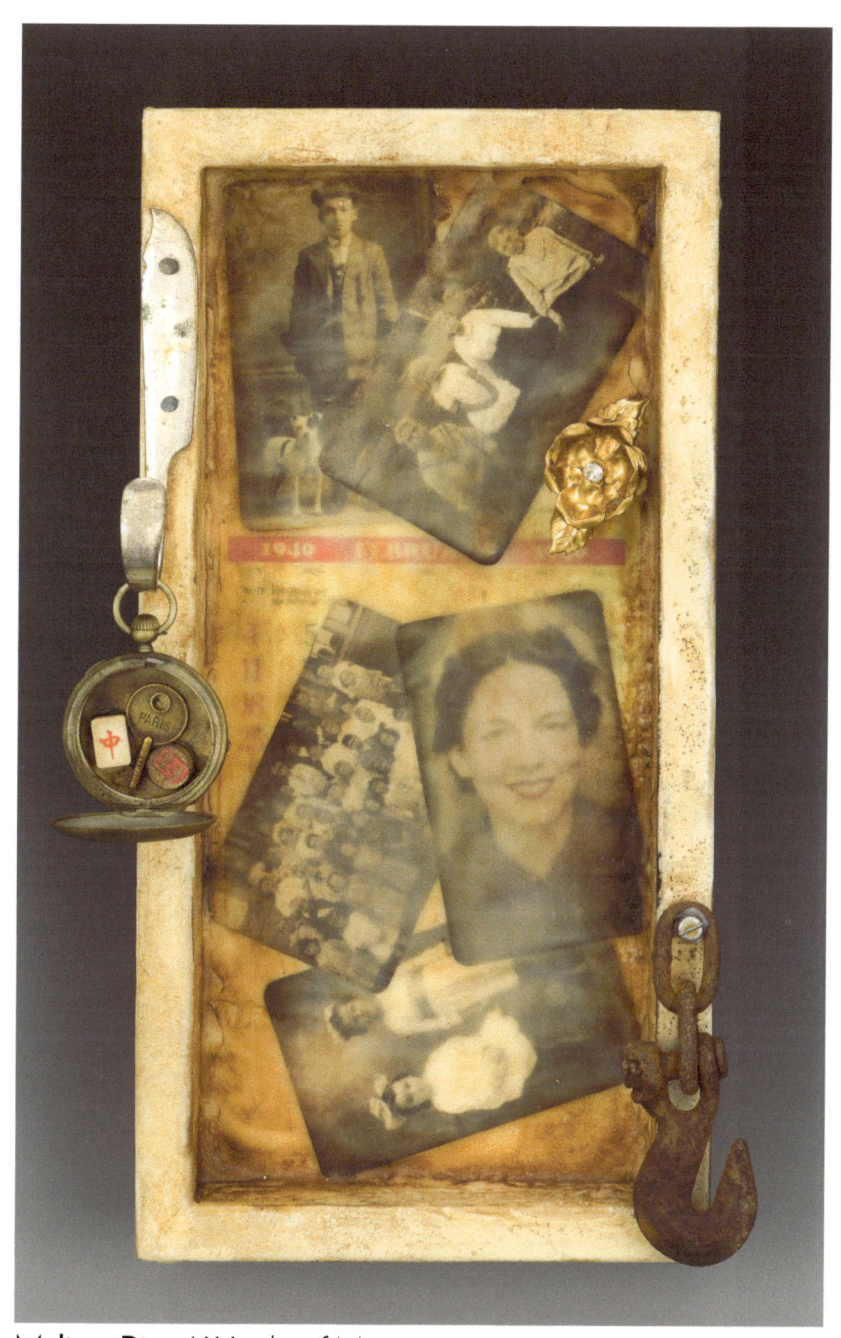

Melissa Rian | Weight of Memory

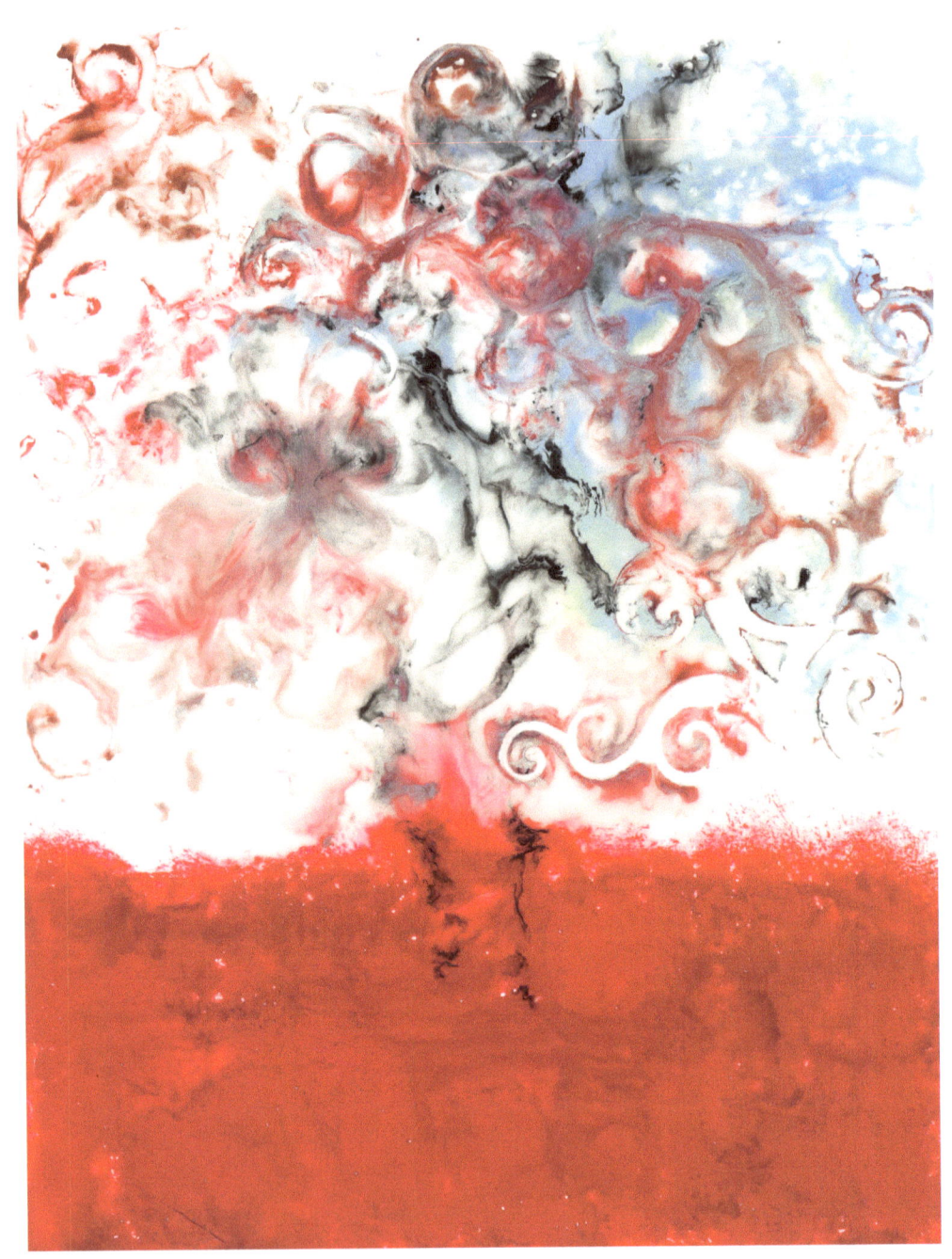

Kathy Jacobi | Spirit Dance

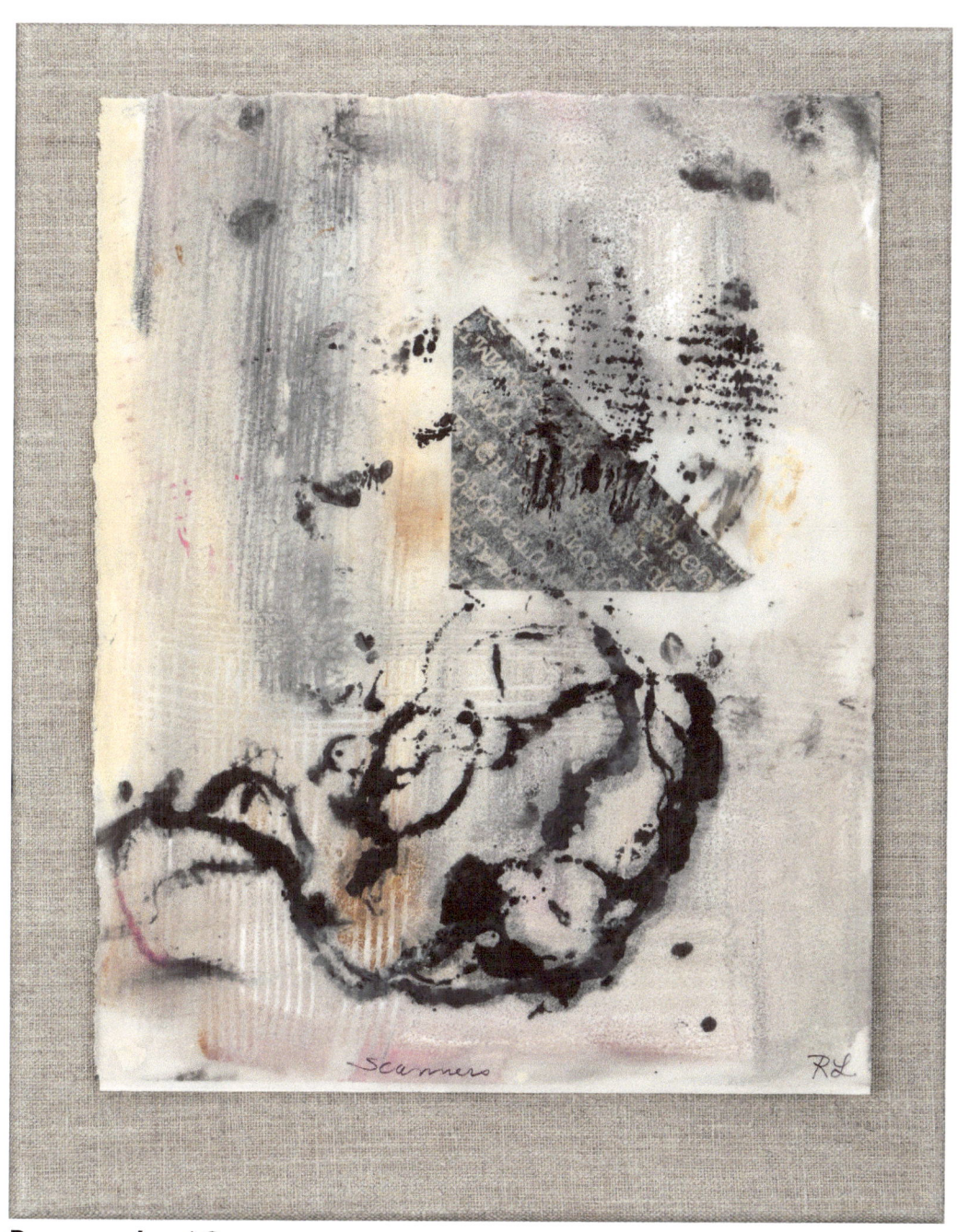

Rosemary Lee | *Scanners*

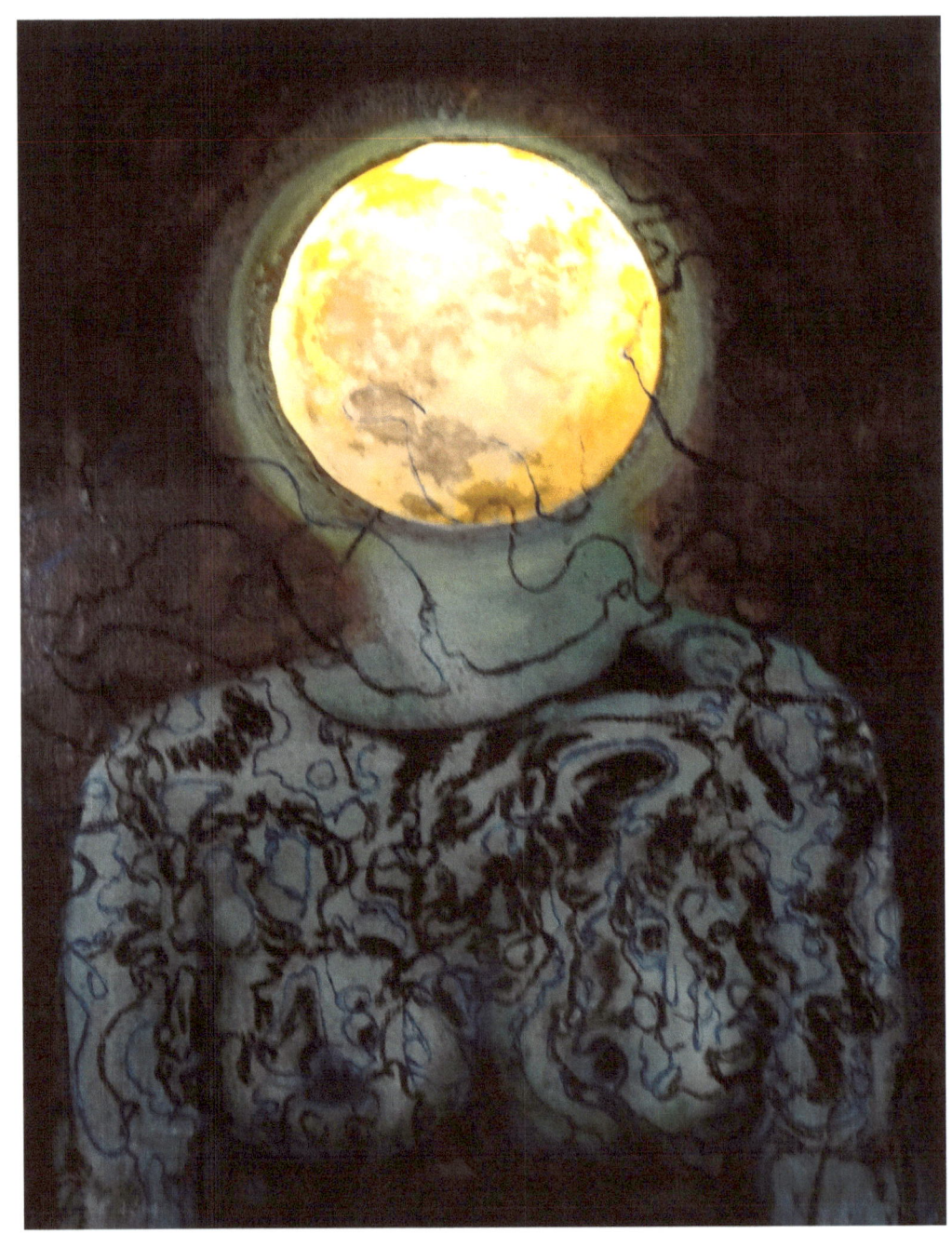

Kate Paul | Moon Tattoo

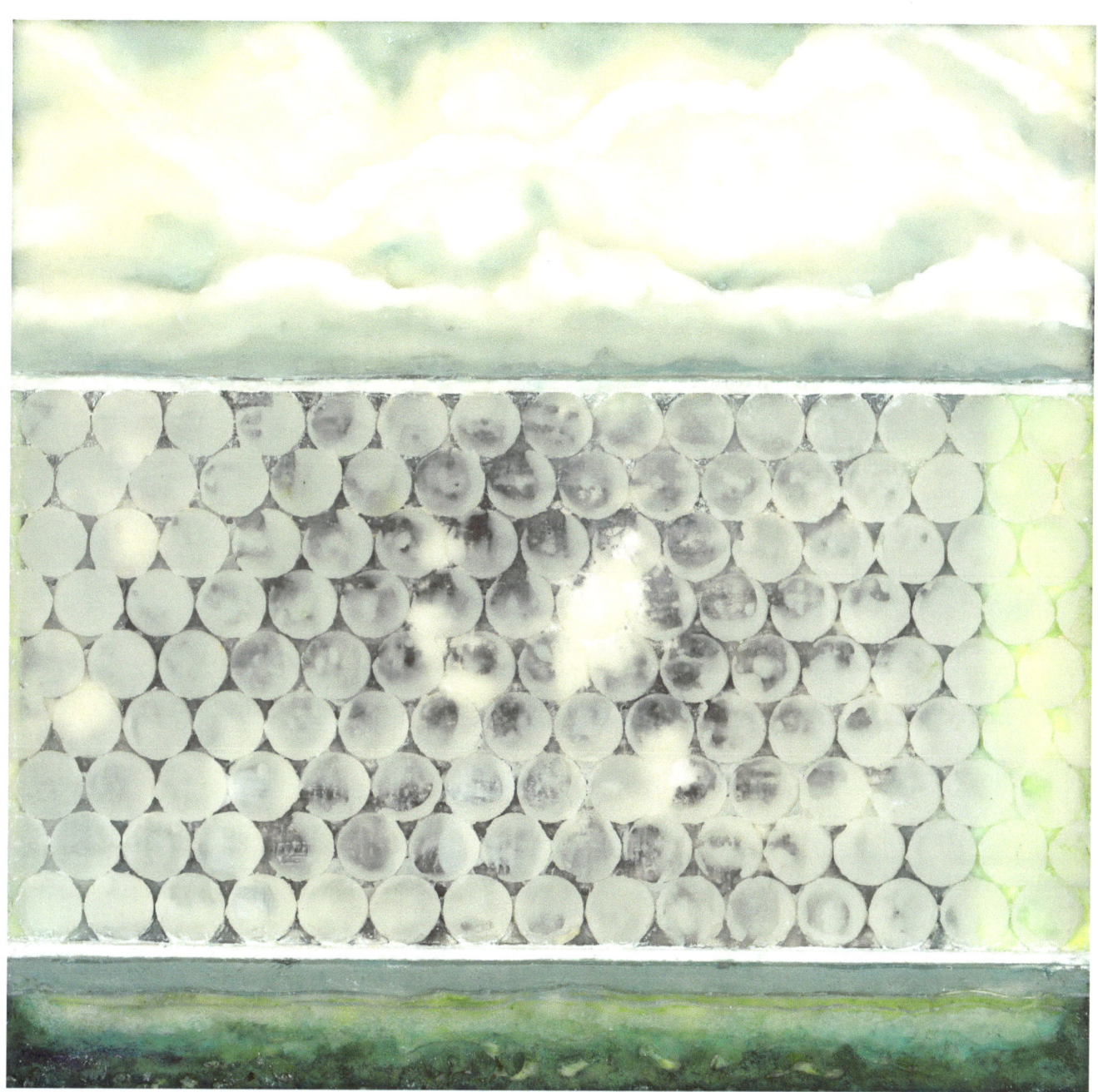

Ruth Warnock | *Sky Garden*

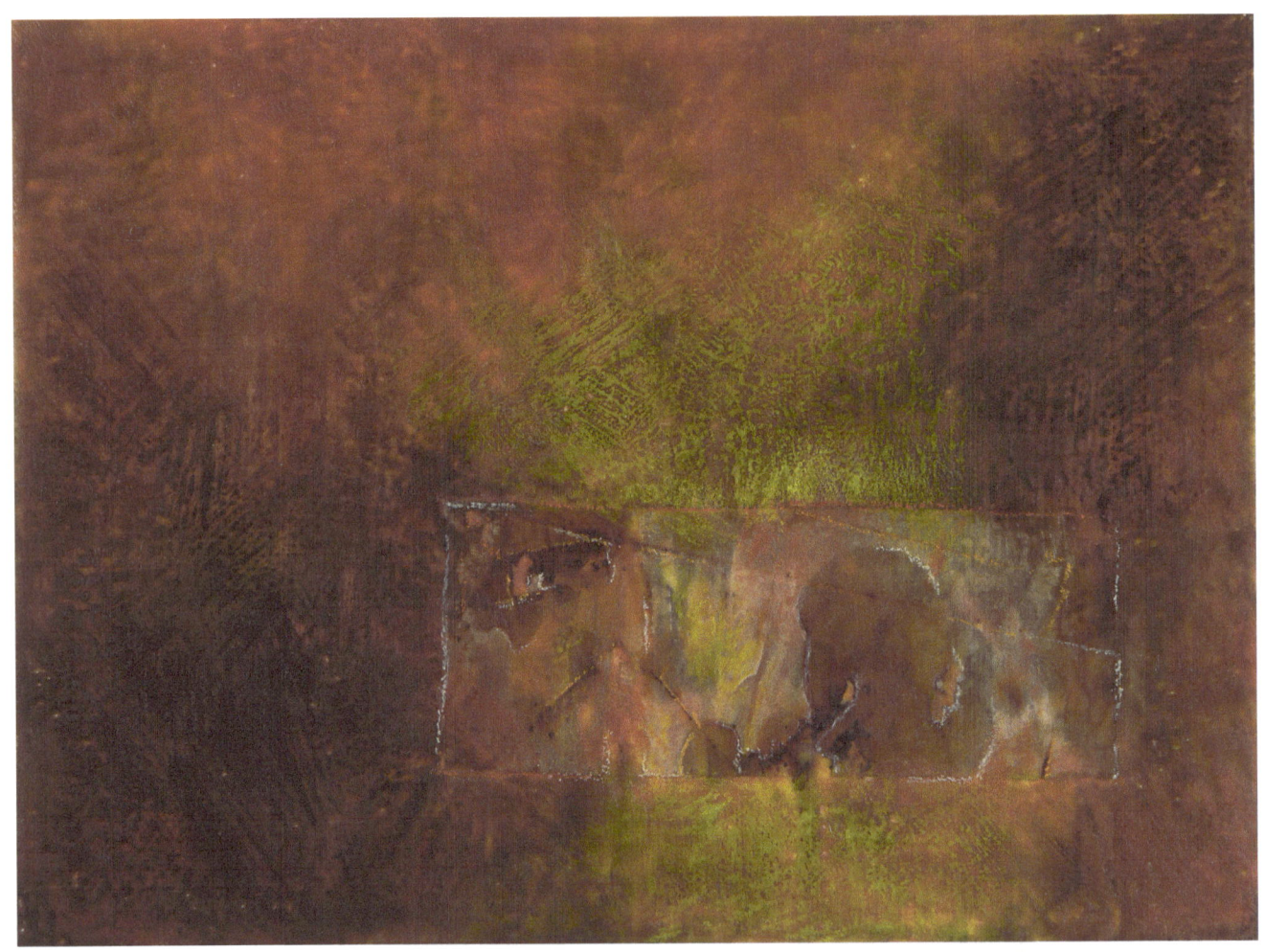

Candace Law | *Ancient Paths*

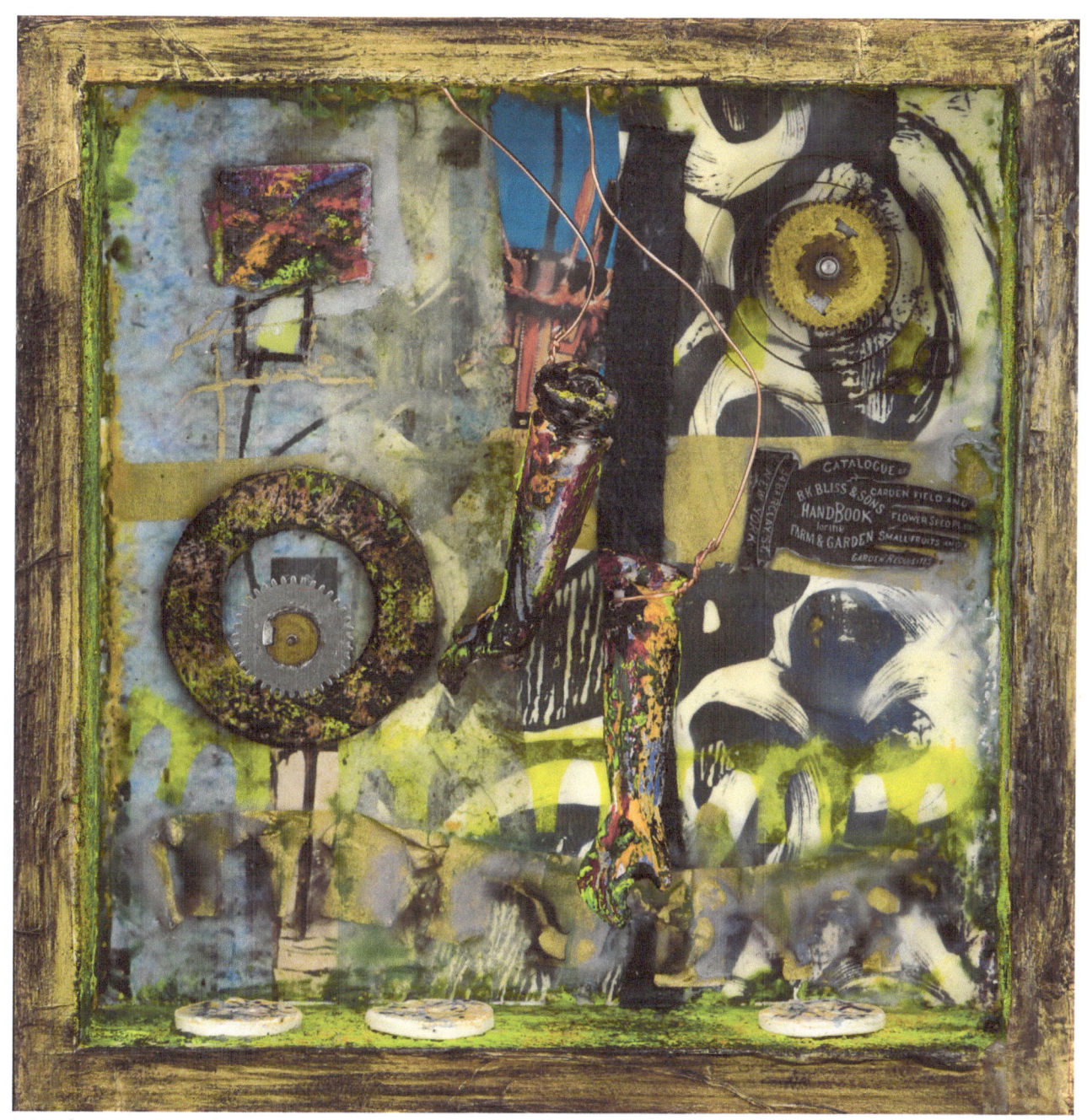

Martha Van Raaphorst | Hands of Time

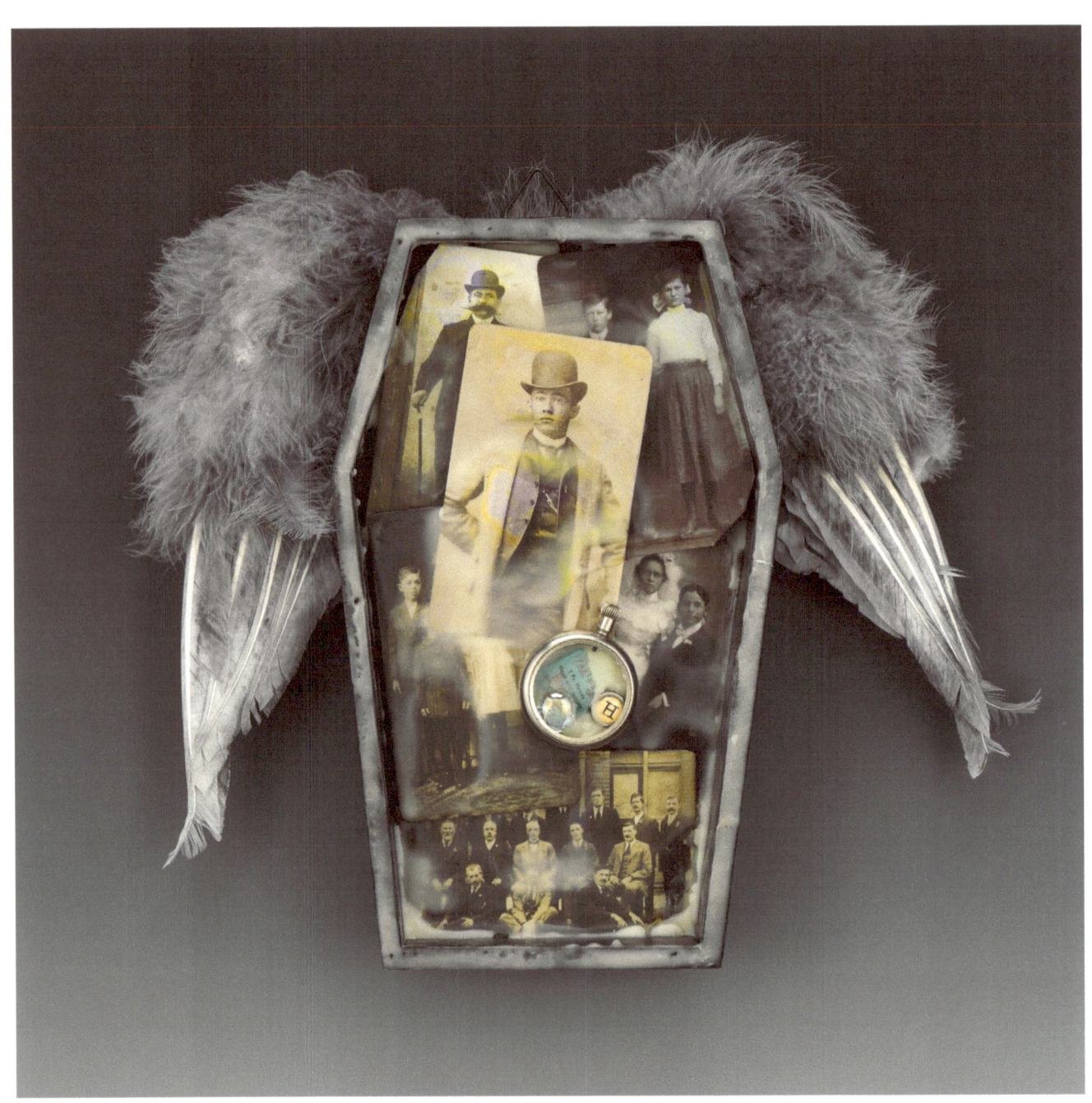

Melissa Rian | Making the Most of It

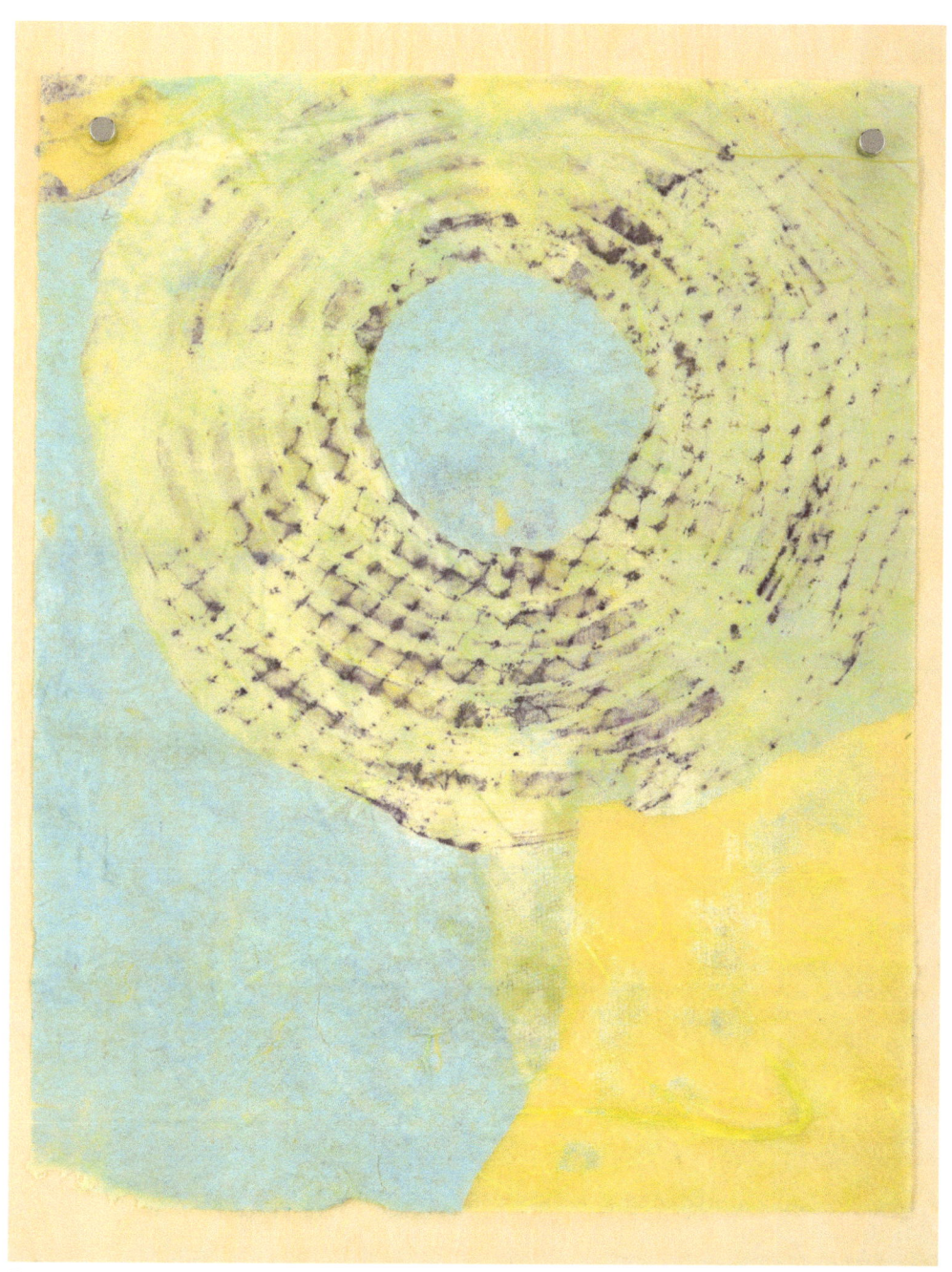

Rosemary Lee | Circular Motion

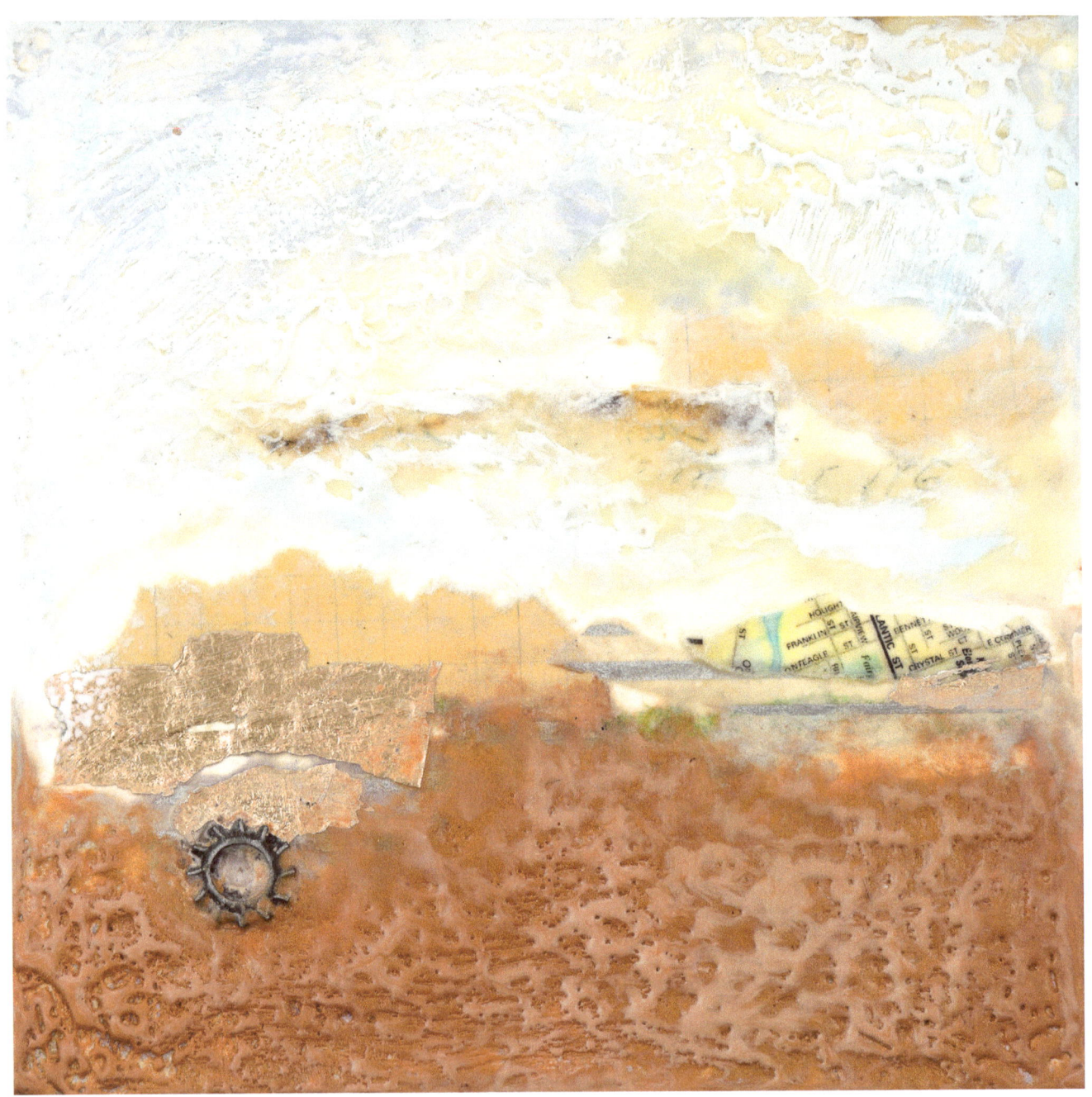

Janice Key | Landscape 2

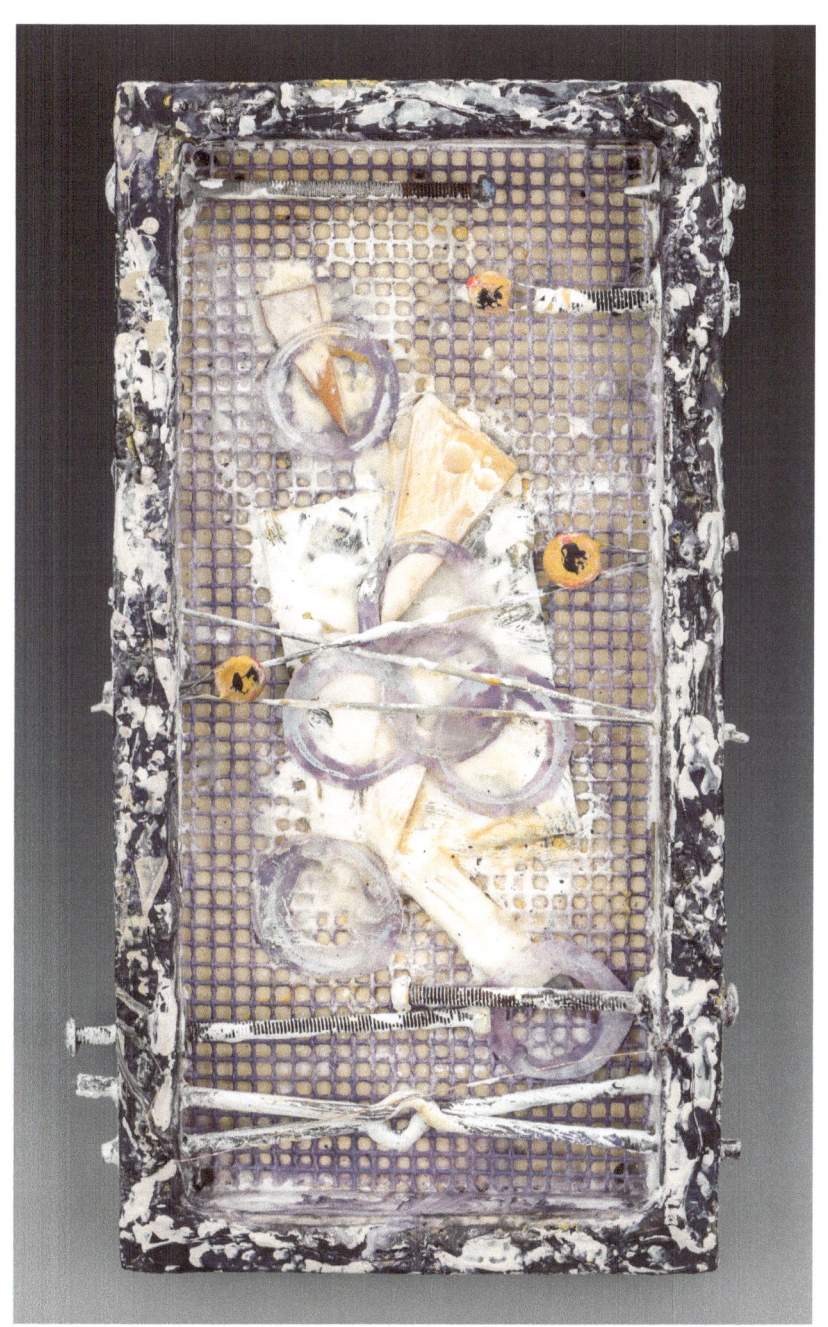

Kim Ensch | Grey and Violet

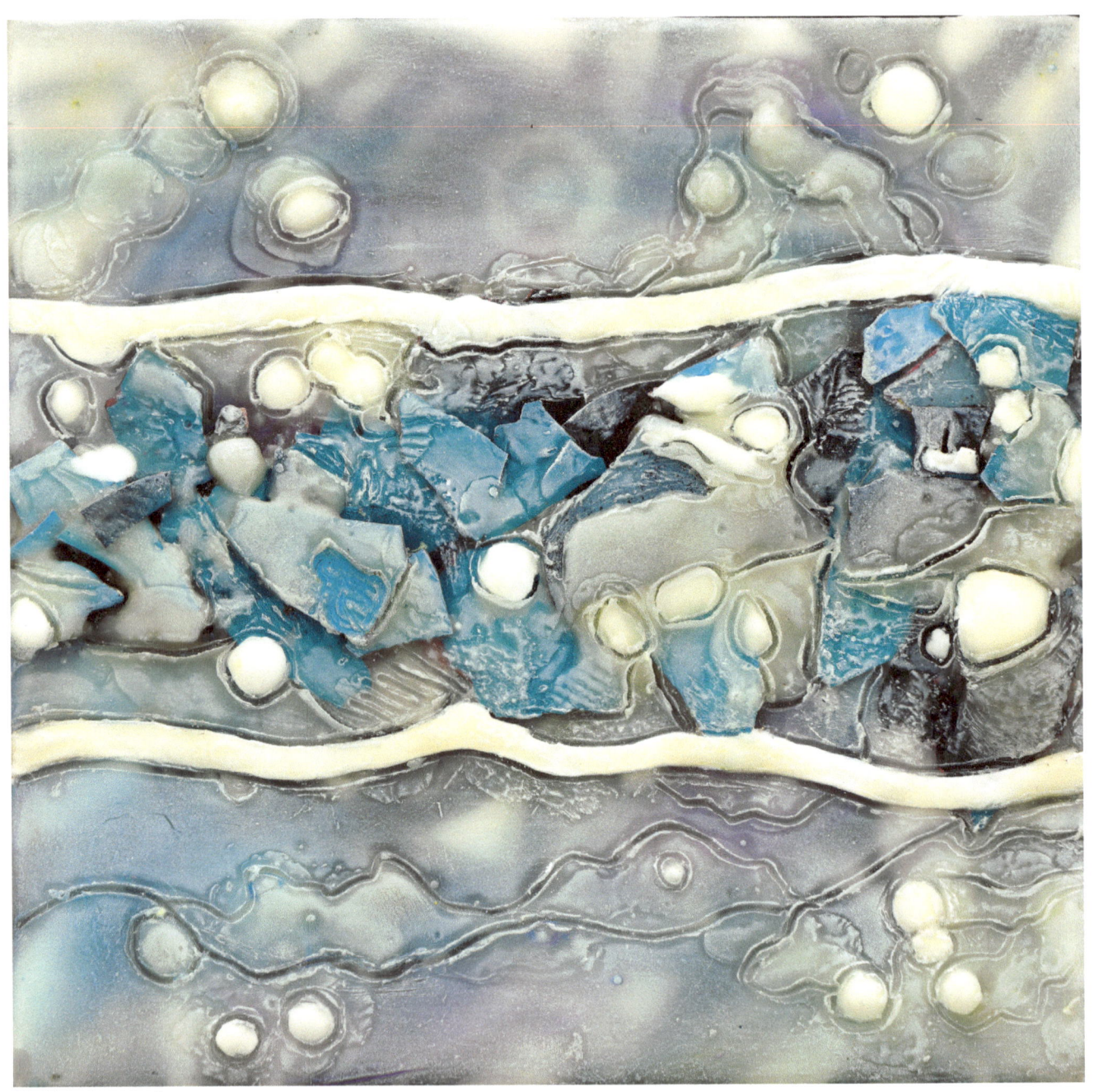

Ruth Warnock | Estuary

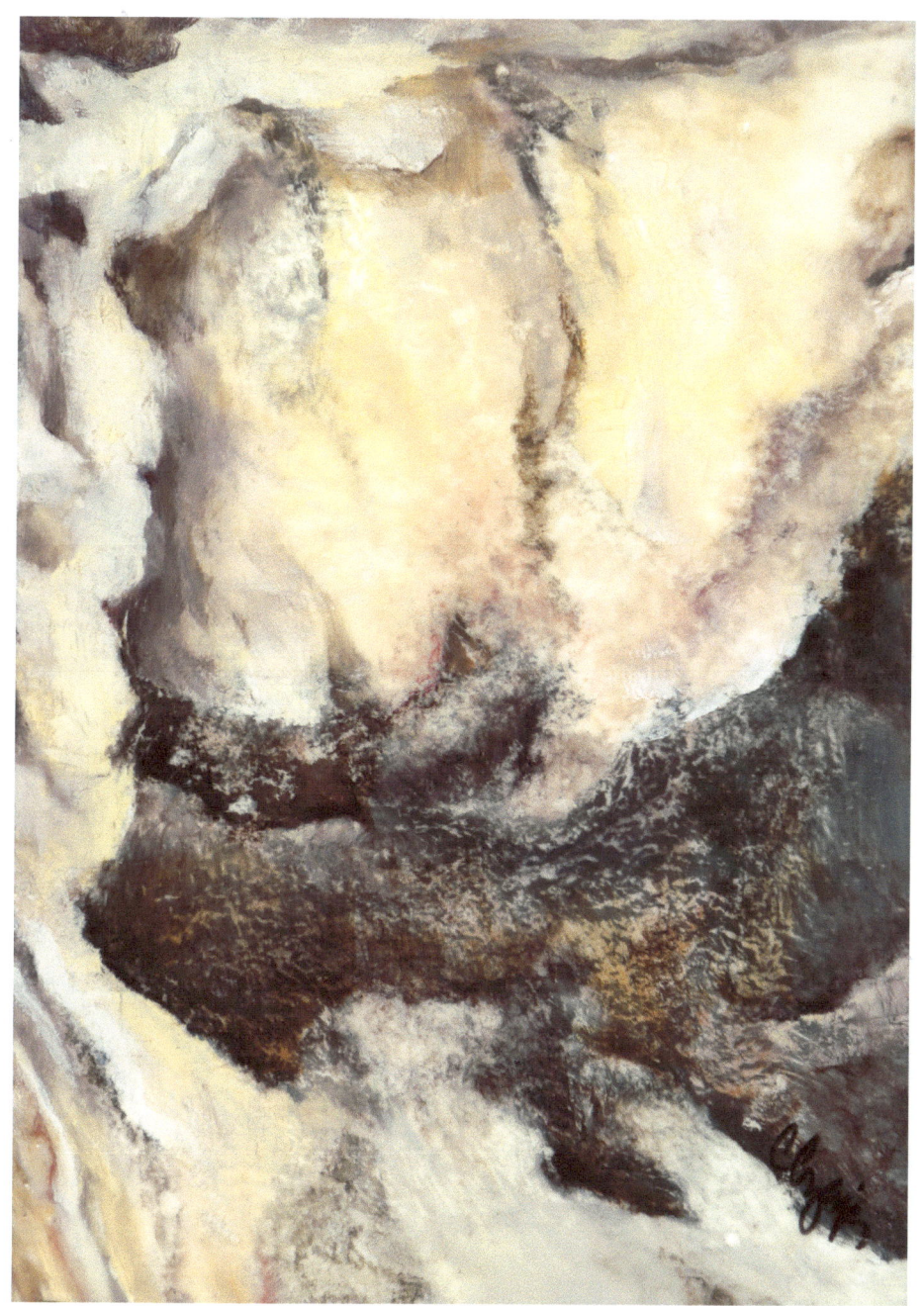

Christina Czaja | Marmore

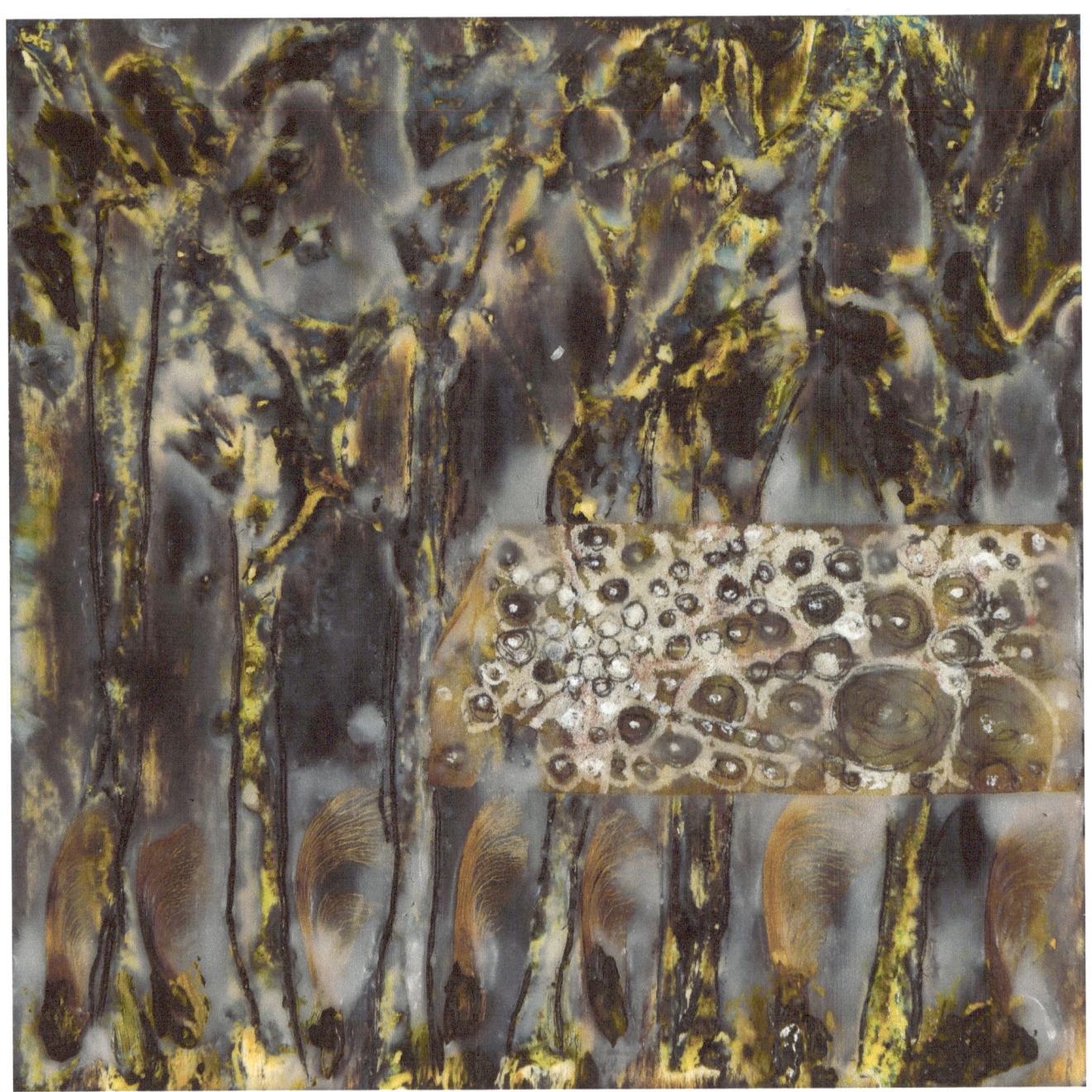

Martha Van Raaphorst | Helicopters Landing

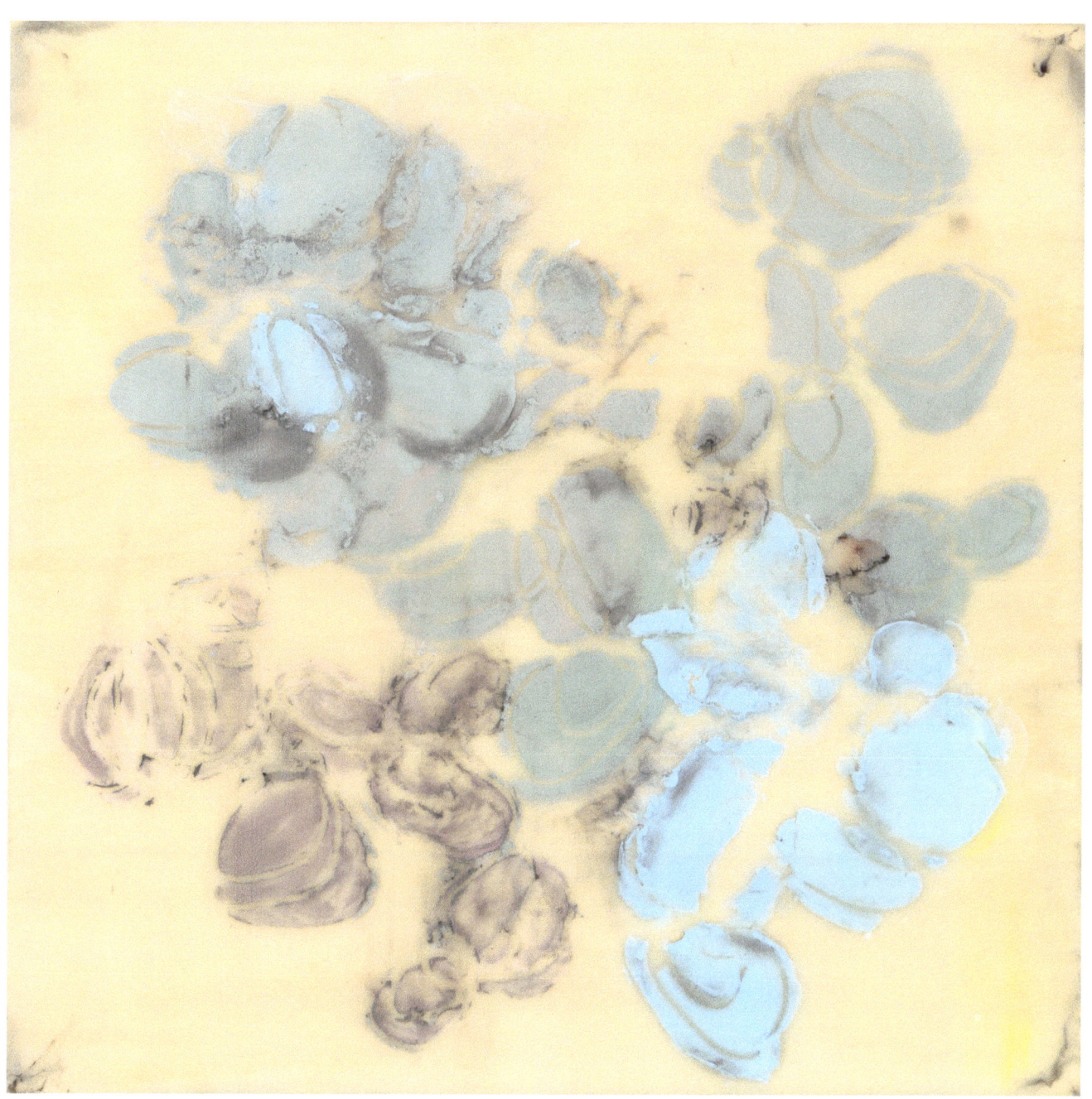

Gwen Downs | Shell Flowers

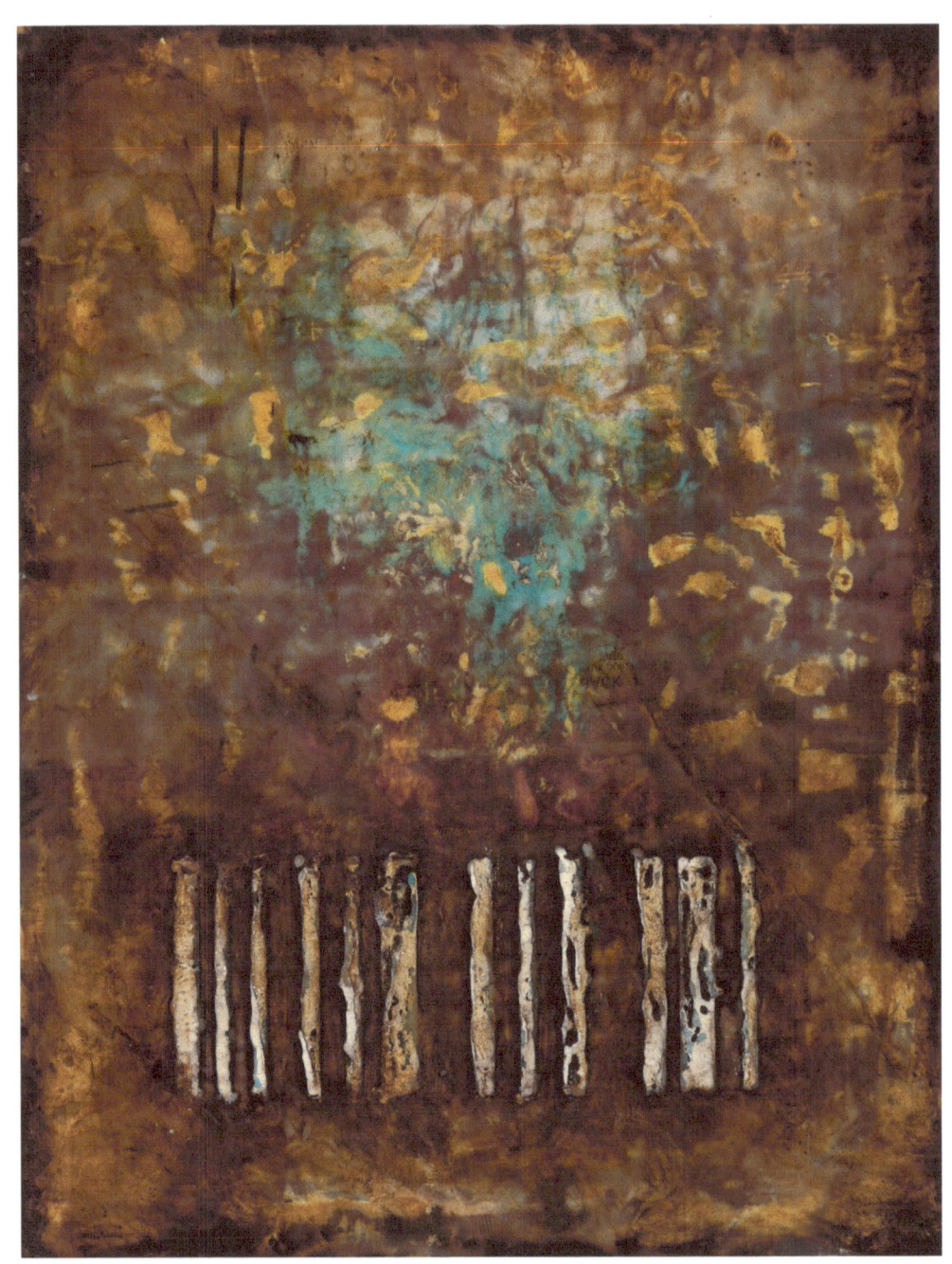

Melissa Rian | Dem Bones

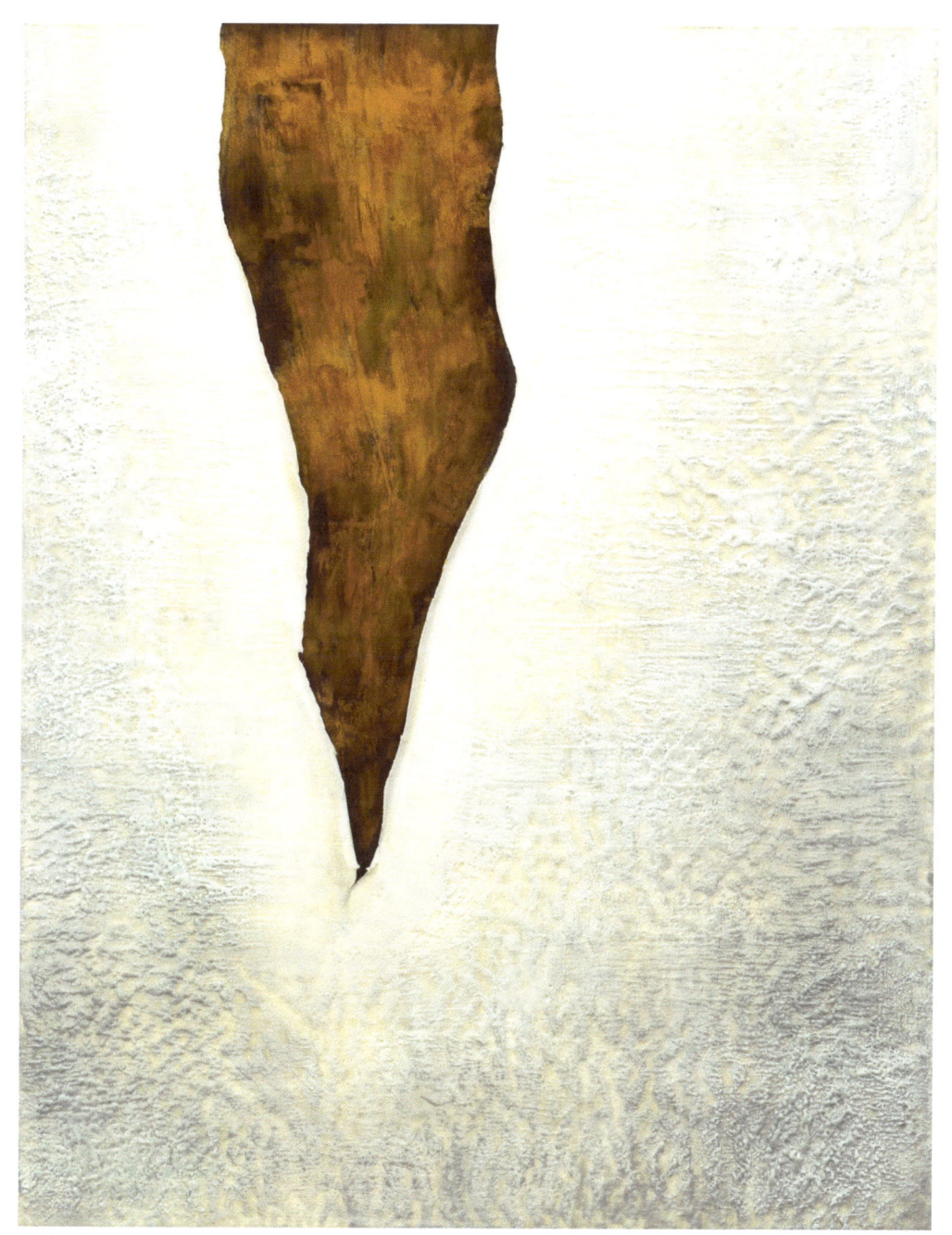

Candace Law | Tectonic

The Artists

Suzanne Allen
Blowing Branches | Encaustic | 10" x 8" | p. 24
Chopstick Temple | Encaustic, Collage, Assemblage | 16" x 8" x 2" | p. 35

Christina Czaja
My Black Abyss | Encaustic, Mixed Media | 7" x 5" | p. 20
Blue Figure | Encaustic, Mixed Media | 6" x 9" | p. 29
Marmore | Encaustic, Mixed Media | 7" x 5" | p. 49

Gwen Downs
Copperscape | Encaustic | 10" x 12" | p. 14
Shell Flowers | Encaustic | 10" x 10" | p. 51

Kim Ensch
Dark Forest | Encaustic, Mixed Media | 8" x 8" | p. 16
Grey Gear | Encaustic, Mixed Media | 8" x 8" | p. 32
Grey and Violet | Encaustic, Assemblage | 16" x 8" x 2" | p. 47

Kathy Jacobi
Last Summer | Encaustic, Collage | 11" x 8" | p. 25
Spirit Dance | Encaustic | 12" x 9" | p. 38

Edee Joppich
Blues Rising | Encaustic | 12" x 12" | p. 13
Where Love Abides | Encaustic, Found Objects | 16" x 8" | p. 28

Janice Key
Landscape 1 | Encaustic, Mixed Media | 6" x 6" | p. 22
Landscape 2 | Encaustic, Mixed Media | 6" x 6" | p. 46

Candace Law
Night of the Soul | Encaustic, Transfer, Mixed Media | 20" x 16" | p. 7
Hide in Plain Sight | Encaustic, Mixed Media, Found Objects | 8" x 10" | p. 17
Unlock | Encaustic, Rust Print, Found Objects | 18" x 14" | p. 30
Wanderings | Encaustic, Mixed Media, Found Objects | 12" x 16" | p. 34
Ancient Paths | Encaustic, Mixed Media | 12" x 16" | p. 42
Tectonic | Encaustic, Rust Print, Torn Paper | 24" x 18" | p. 53

Rosemary Lee
On the Written Word | Encaustic Monotype | 8" x 8" | p. 10
Scanners | Encaustic Monotype | 14" x 11" | p. 39
Circular Motion | Monotype, Encaustic Medium | 12" x 9" | p. 45

Nora Chapa Mendoza
City Scape | Encaustic, Assemblage on Cello Front | 17" x 30" x 6" | p. 11

Kate Paul
Ledger | Green Teabag Paper, Encaustic | 12" x 24" | p. 9
Storm Rise | Charcoal, Image Transfer, Encaustic | 24" x 24" | p. 26
Moon Tattoo | Oil Paint, Ink, Silk, LED Lighting, Encaustic Medium | 24" x 18" | p. 40

Melissa Rian
No Fly Zone | Encaustic, Assemblage | 10" x 4" x 1½" | p. 18
The Egg Came First | Encaustic, Assemblage | 18" x 6" x 6" | p. 23
Commitment Ceremony | Encaustic, Photo Transfer | 20" x 16" | p. 27
Natures Trophy | Encaustic, Assemblage | 13" x 5" x 1" | p. 33
Weight of Memory | Encaustic, Assemblage | 16" x 10" x 4" | p. 37
Making the Most of It | Encaustic, Assemblage | 13" x 14" x 3" | p. 44
Dem Bones | Encaustic | 16" x 12" | p. 52

Martha Van Raaphorst
Blue Heaven | Encaustic, Mixed Media | 10" x 8" | p. 12
Once Upon a Spring | Encaustic monotype on Japanese Paper | 13" x 9" | p. 21

Martha Van Raaphorst (continued)

Ruth Warnock

Wendy Wernet

Visit WaxintheD.com to see more artwork by these and other artists.

The Curator

Candace Law is a full time artist in the Detroit area. After receiving degrees and working in other fields, she earned a BFA in Architectural Illustration, but found herself drawn to fine art. Her current body of work focuses on encaustic (hot wax) and mixed media, especially incorporating found objects. "Art for me is a means of communicating about our environment, our lives, sharing our experiences, and reflecting how they inform each other." Her exhibits include several solo shows as well as numerous regional and national exhibitions—both invitational and juried competitions. Her work has appeared in Encaustic Arts magazine, as well as the Studio Visit publication, and is in a number of private collections, including at Detroit's Historic Trinity Church. Candace teaches encaustic workshops and works from her studio in Berkley, Michigan.

www.ingramcontent.com/pod-product-compliance
Lightning Source LLC
Chambersburg PA
CBHW050807180526
45159CB00004B/1582